For Susi and Ollie, with love

Contents

Preface

I regularly used to wake in a panic from a recurring nightmare in which I was the survivor of a nuclear holocaust. In the nightmare I belonged to a small band of survivors, each of whom was given a task to help towards the reconstruction of Western civilization. My job was to make a summary of philosophical ideas from ancient Greece to the present, which would be used in the rebuilt universities to teach the first generation of post-Armageddon philosophy students. Little did I know that this recurring nightmare was actually a premonition of the day when Richard Milbank would phone from Atlantic Books to ask if I would do exactly that.

Writers enjoy phone calls of the commissioning kind, so naturally I said yes straight away. 'Oh good,' I thought, 'this is like a dream come true.' The next morning I awoke in a blind panic with that old, familiar post-nightmare feeling . . . It soon passed. I rolled up my sleeves and set about organizing my task.

At the end of the day, it seemed to me, the history of philosophy boiled down to one basic question: what can we *know*? And that question is framed in the context of another: what do we *believe*? The first philosophers, it seemed to me, were concerned to separate knowledge from belief. They would do this, for instance, by replacing creation myths with a scientific explanation of how our world came to be.

The tension between belief (or faith) and knowledge (or reason) is as powerful today as it was in the time of Socrates. A 2010 Gallup poll found that 40 per cent of Americans believe that God created the world in six days; 38 per cent believe we evolved from more basic organisms, but that God played a part in the process; 16 per cent subscribe to the science-based, evolutionary evidence that human beings evolved over a long period of time. How long? Radiocarbon dating is accurate to 58,000 to 62,000 years. The fossil record dates *Homo sapiens* as being 200,000 years old (although they only acquired full human functionality about 50,000 years ago). Creationists argue that not only *Homo sapiens* but the entire world is only somewhere between 6,000 and 10,000 years old. However, the latest scientific measurement, taken from microwaves released during the Big Bang, shows the universe to be 13.75 billion years old. Science and religion are not necessarily incompatible: many scientists have been (and are today) believers. But erroneous belief and science *are* incompatible. Defining the difference between knowing and believing is philosophy's first task.

Of course, philosophy is about complex ideas and arguments, and in writing this popular history it might be objected by some that I have made generalizations or that I have failed to do justice to one or another school of thought. On the other hand, the general reader has every right to make acquaintance with some of the greatest philosophers of the past, and to be offered some introduction to the key thinkers of today. The philosophers Immanuel Kant, Blaise Pascal and Henri Bergson were all great mathematicians, but they also managed to convey their philosophical ideas in a language that ordinary readers could understand.

Philosophy is our best means of sorting good ideas from bad, so it has always been a competitive pursuit. This is also why philosophy can be stubbornly sectarian. Modern philosophy, for instance, is split between the analytic and continental camps. The analytic philosopher A. J. Ayer didn't mince his words. He considered the work of the philosophers Martin Heidegger and Jean-Paul Sartre to be, quite literally, meaningless (he really did mean that their work didn't mean anything). For my part, I disagree with Ayer, while finding his work engaging and amusing, his prose brisk, and his ideas to have meaning (though their meaning may quite possibly be wrong). I also find much that I can agree with in Heidegger and Sartre, as well as plenty I cannot agree with.

But we are getting ahead of our story. In this book I have tried to give a brief overview of some of the key moments in Western philosophy, from the time of the Presocratics (around the sixth century BC) to the present day. My hope is that I have been able to convey at least some of the joy and excitement I have felt in revisiting our great philosophical tradition.

What is Philosophy?

What is philosophy? Even some philosophers argue that it doesn't exist in its own right. As long ago as the seventeenth century the German mathematician and logician Joachim Jung (1587–1657) said it is 'completely dependent on material delivered by various scientific, scholarly or cultural activities. Philosophy does not have any resources of its own at its disposal.' But that is merely one view. More optimistically, the Frenchmen Gilles Deleuze (1925–95) and Félix Guattari (1930–92) described it as 'the art of forming, inventing and fabricating concepts' (*What Is Philosophy?*, 1991). According to the Spanish American philosopher George Santayana (1863–1952) it is 'a gradual mastering of experience by reason' (*The Life of Reason*, 1905–6). Before that, the German phenomenologist Max Scheler (1874–1928) called it 'a love-determined movement of the inmost personal self of a finite being toward participation in the essential reality of all possibles' (*On the Eternal in Man*, 1960). But way before any of these, the Greek philosopher Aristotle (384–322 BC) simply said that it begins with *wonder*.

PART ONE

The Wisdom of the Ancients

6th century BC to 1st century AD

The first philosophers were called Presocratics, because they worked in the period before the Greek philosopher Socrates (*c.*469–399 BC), from about 585 BC to 400 BC. The prefix *pre-* tells us that Socrates is a chronological marker indicating a change in thought. There is a *before* Socrates and an *after* – the before period is popularly understood as being characterized by a fragmented approach to knowledge, with the after Socrates period constituting a more systematic and sophisticated approach. But the work of the Presocratics might seem more fragmented than what came after only because the evidence we have of it is fragmentary. Very few original texts remain, and most of our knowledge of Presocratic thought is filtered through the verbal accounts, translations – and therefore prejudices – of those that followed.

For philosophy (and I include here the concepts of *thought* and *thinking* in general), the Socratic moment is important in the way that the moment represented by the birth of Jesus Christ (*c.*5 BC–*c.*AD 30) is important. The establishment of Christ's birth as the year zero of Western civilization trumps the Socratic moment, for it determined that time and history would henceforth be regarded as Anno Domini (AD), 'in the year of the Lord', the past being referred to as Before Christ (BC). Socrates and Jesus Christ the man (Socrates made no claim to divinity!) had several things in common: both were teachers; both were executed for their beliefs; both left behind schools of followers who would guarantee the longevity of their ideas; and both abided by a one-word commandment. For Socrates it was *think*; for Christ, *love*.

Socrates' disadvantage

One advantage Socrates had over the Presocratics is that his thought was recorded by his pupil Plato (*c.*428/7–*c.*348/7 BC) and so survives intact to this day. The disadvantage that Socrates, Aristotle and the other Greek fathers of Western philosophy endured is that their light was hidden under a bushel for more than a thousand years, while Christian thought prospered and became dominant.

A fact that might annoy contemporary Islamophobes is that we owe our knowledge of the Greek philosophers to Islamic scholars who transcribed their texts into Arabic at a time when the Greek tongue had been lost in the West as a result of the dominance of Latin, the language of the Roman Empire.

Arabic translators preserved classical thought, and it is from their texts that the Greeks eventually found their way into Latin in the twelfth century, and into the vernacular during the fifteenth and sixteenth centuries. It is remarkable to note that the first complete English translations of Plato and Aristotle (384–322 BC) did not appear until the nineteenth century. They were made by Thomas Taylor (1758–1835), and published posthumously in 1804 (Plato), and between 1806 and 1812 (Aristotle).

The Presocratics: wonder and wealth

The Presocratic philosophers were driven by the wonder that Aristotle describes as the chief motivator in philosophy. When I wonder, I do many things. I wonder about how the stars came to be in the sky – that is, I ask questions about how and why there are stars in the sky. Looking at the sky I am in a state of wonder as I behold its vastness; I am wonderstruck, yet I want to know: how big is the universe? I may also be filled with doubt: I may wonder if so-and-so's explanation of how the stars got there is correct. My doubt may even extend to wondering if my own explanation is correct.

The Greek city-state of Miletus – on the western coast of Anatolia in what is now modern Turkey – was the birthplace of Western thought in the sense that the first Presocratic philosophers lived there. Among the most famous were Thales (*c*.624–*c*.546 BC), Anaximander (*c*.610–*c*.546 BC), and Anaximenes (*c*.585–*c*.528 BC). While it is tempting to group thinkers together into 'schools', or to ascribe some common preoccupation among them, at the end of the day all that can said with any certainty is that these early men of ideas lived in the same place at the same time.

If we were to wonder why our Western tradition of thought began at Miletus, we could do worse than to notice the geographical position of that city: it was on a trade route that linked it with the cultures of Babylon, Lydia, Egypt and Phoenicia. As the classicist Robin Waterfield has remarked in *The First Philosophers* (2000), 'ideas always travel with trade'. We might also notice something about philosophy (and philosophers) that is true from the very start: it is an occupation of the leisured – and, therefore, wealthy – classes. The association of wealth with ideas is dominant right into the modern period: Michel de Montaigne's (1533–92) father was an extremely successful trader; Søren Kierkegaard's (1813–55) was a rich wool merchant; Isaac Newton's (1643–1727) family were rich landowners; Ludwig Wittgenstein (1889–1951) came from one of the wealthiest families in Europe; Bertrand Russell (1872–1970) from one of the noblest in England; A. J. Ayer's (1910–89) mother was a member of the Citroën family, the eponymous French car manufacturer.

The Greek philosopher was a wealthy, upper-class man whose leisure time was purchased with slave labour. So, with some exceptions, philosophy was a male profession from which women were excluded. One such exception was Theano (sixth century BC), who may have been the wife of Pythagoras (*c*.570–*c*.495 BC), and whose school was said to contain twenty-eight women. We can compare the situation of philosophy in ancient Greece with our own time, in which – despite the fact that more philosophers may be women or people of colour or come from modest social origins – it remains a profession dominated by white men.

Thales: philosopher and scientist

Thales was the quintessential Presocratic thinker. He was more than 'just' a philosopher; he was an engineer, a mathematician and a scientist. Increasingly, the philosophers of our own age are specialists who cultivate a very narrow patch of knowledge that is of interest only to other professional philosophers (which, lucky for them perhaps, is a surprisingly large number – more than 10,000 worldwide). But every now and again a person is born with the wonder and the intellectual wherewithal to be a philosopher like Thales; in modern times, the American C. S. Peirce (1839–1914) comes to mind.

Thales was regarded as something of a wizard by his contemporaries, for he correctly predicted the solar eclipse of 28 May 585 BC. (In fact, he predicted a range of dates *within* the year 585 BC, not the precise date.) During these early years of philosophy, an epistemological sea change was taking place, a move from mythology-based belief systems to a systematic use of reason to acquire knowledge. However, this was known only to a very small group that comprised philosophers themselves, their students and their friends. The shift from belief to knowledge occurred over a very long period of time, and it involved a minority of people, because of the hierarchical structure of Athenian society. The slaves who made up a significant portion of the population in ancient Greece were not educated, and nor were most of the 51 per cent of Greeks who were women. So, while Thales' prediction of the solar eclipse of 585 BC was based more on science than superstition, most people would not have appreciated the difference.

How did Thales predict the eclipse? Babylonian astronomers had kept a record of eclipses called the Saros cycle. There was also a second, more accurate cycle called the Exeligmos cycle, and it is likely that Thales knew both of them. In examining such records Thales was doing what most scientists do every day of their working lives: that is, bench science, working with experimental data and the observations of other scientists, moving knowledge along inch by inch.

But Thales was also doing wholly original philosophy when he asked the question: what is the primary principle at work in the world? What is the one thing that is irreducible? His answer was *water*. For Thales, water is the substance from which everything originates, and to which everything returns. In water Thales saw the kinds of transformations into different states – solid, liquid, gas – that would account for many other natural phenomena.

> Thales says that the world is held up by water and rides on it like a ship, and what we call an earthquake happens when the earth rocks because of the movement of the water.
>
> Seneca, *Questions about Nature* (c.AD 65)
>
> (trans. Robin Waterfield, 2000)

Thales was important because he sought to explain the natural world without reference to gods. He replaced the divine with the physical. He proposed that the stuff of the universe was one primary, organizing substance. He set off a tradition that made the search for one irreducible substance a kind of grail quest in philosophy. Aristotle would later say that several substances exist in their own right, without being dependent upon any others. But the Presocratics wanted one ultimate substance and it was variously proposed to be water, fire, air or earth. Thales' contemporary Anaximander contributed the wholly original concept of *apeiron*, which translates as 'without limits' or 'boundless'. Like many philosophical concepts that would follow, *apeiron* was mysterious and hard to grasp. Sometimes, philosophers are praised for their precision and clarity; such diverse figures as John Stuart Mill (1806–73) and William James (1842–1910) would be good examples. And then again, philosophers are sometimes prized for their opacity: the German Martin Heidegger (1889–1976) is a fine twentieth-century example; he and Anaximander would have made good colleagues.

Ultimately, Christian philosophers of the medieval period would replace the natural concept of ultimate substance with that of God; later still, G. W. F. Hegel (1770–1831) would posit the Absolute or Spirit as the ultimate substance.

Anaximander says that the first living creatures were born in a moist medium, surrounded by thorny barks . . .

Aëtius (*c.*396–454), *Opinions*
(trans. Robin Waterfield, 2000)

Four elements, four humours: philosophy, medicine and the Presocratic worldview

Thales' contemporary Anaximenes thought fire was the ultimate substance, but one that could be transformed in various ways to become earth, air or water, thus accounting for all four elements. The concept of the element is an enduring one, as can be seen from the periodic table first proposed in 1869 by the Russian chemist Dmitri Mendeleev (1834–1907). In 1789 the Frenchman Antoine Lavoisier (1743–94), who is sometimes called the father of modern chemistry, had published a list of 33 chemical elements. Mendeleev's periodic table now contains 118 of them. But the Greeks had just four elements, and these would correspond to the four *humours* of Greek medicine as developed by Hippocrates (*c*.470–*c*.360 BC).

Hippocrates is the father of Western medicine and his most enduring legacy is the Hippocratic Oath, which is still sworn by new doctors in the twenty-first century. The oath is ascribed to Hippocrates, although it might have been composed by another – some claim it was written by followers of Pythagoras. No matter, for it is the spirit of the oath that counts: 'In every house where I come I will enter only for the good of my patients.' But the Hippocratic Oath is more than a promise not to harm present and future patients; it is also a promise to honour the past teachers from whom physicians had received their knowledge. It is the document that best summarizes the value that ancient Greeks placed on learning: 'To consider dear to me, as my parents, him who taught me this art; to live in common with him and, if necessary, to share my goods with him; to look upon his children as my own brothers, to teach them this art.'

The development of medicine and the rise of philosophy in ancient Greece are contemporaneous, and the researches of physicians and philosophers inform one another. For instance, the concept of the four elements finds a correspondence in the four humours by which Hippocrates understood the human body and which he used to diagnose and treat ailments. The four humours or basic elements of the human body were *black bile, yellow bile, phlegm* and *blood*. It is worth pausing to look at the relationship of these concepts with those of the four elements of air, fire, earth, and water, because it constitutes what mid-nineteenth-century German philosophers would come to describe as a *Weltanschauung* or *worldview*. A worldview is an orientation towards the world that is shared by a large number of people at a given time; it is the way a society or group views the world, and it reflects the knowledge, beliefs, traditions, theoretical tendencies and prejudices that determine the way in which the world is understood. In the period before the Presocratics, the prevailing worldview was mythological. Starting in the seventeenth century, the scientific worldview arose and challenged that of the Church (we find, again, a conflict between knowledge and belief).

Prayer is a good thing, but one should take on part of the burden oneself and call on the gods only to help.

Hippocrates (*c.*470–*c.*360 BC), *Dreams*

(trans. J. Chadwick and W. N. Mann, 1950)

The worldview developed by the Presocratics was a complex mix of metaphysics and science, as can be seen from the humoral pathology of Hippocrates and his followers (who followed him all the way into the nineteenth century, until experimental science and medical technology developed sufficiently to replace Hippocratic ideas). The four humours of blood, yellow bile, black bile and phlegm corresponded, in order, to a range of organizational and conceptual quartets. The corresponding elements were air, fire, earth and water. The temporal correspondences were spring, summer, autumn and winter. The four humours corresponded to the organs thought to govern health: the liver, gall bladder and spleen, with phlegm doing double duty governing both brain and lungs. Qualities were associated with the four humours: warm and moist (blood); warm and dry (yellow bile); cold and dry (black bile); and cold and moist (phlegm). Four temperaments are identified with the humours: sanguine (blood);

choleric (yellow bile); melancholic (black bile); and phlegmatic (phlegm). Apart from melancholic (sad, suffering from melancholy), the human characteristics ascribed to the humours have fallen out of common usage. But, up until the Second World War it was not uncommon to hear someone described as sanguine (healthy, optimistic), choleric (passionate, angry) or phlegmatic (calm, unemotional).

Homer to Heraclitus: the emergence of the soul

The clash of religious belief and philosophy took a new turn with Xenophanes (*c*.570–*c*.475 BC) who roundly rejected the prevailing religion that was based on the poetry of Homer, who is thought to have flourished around 850 BC, and was the author of the epic poems the *Iliad* and the *Odyssey*. Homer's religion was populated by gods who lived on Mount Olympus and were ruled by Zeus. The gods were immortal and had human form. Xenophanes dispensed with Homer's polytheistic, anthropomorphic religion and replaced it with a single god who, while he might be embodied, did not take human form. Xenophanes influenced Heraclitus (*c*.535–*c*.475 BC), though not other contemporaries. Xenophanes' cosmology was not as sophisticated as those of his fellow Presocratics, but he did introduce the idea that the earth had once been covered with mud, and would be again.

As evidence of this he cited marine fossils that he discovered inland – the type of fieldwork that in a later age would lead Charles Darwin (1809–82) to develop his theory of evolution and the origin of species.

> To this universal Reason which I unfold, although it always exists, men make themselves insensible, both before they have heard it and when they have heard it for the first time. For notwithstanding that all things happen according to this Reason, men act as though they had never had any experience in regard to it when they attempt such words and works as I am now relating, describing each thing according to its nature and explaining how it is ordered. And some men are as ignorant of what they do when awake as they are forgetful of what they do when asleep.
>
> Heraclitus, *Fragments* (trans. G. T. W. Patrick, 1889)

Of the four elements, it was fire that most fascinated Heraclitus. His fragments are full of images of war and fire. He not only believed that the soul was animated by fire, he is also thought to have concluded that the world was periodically consumed in a fiery conflagration.

Heraclitus was the first philosopher to identify the self with a soul, rather than the body. His manner was prophetic, a quality exaggerated by his key concept, which he called the *logos*. The literal translation of *logos* is *word*, but Heraclitus means more than that. He talks of wisdom as being the ability to open oneself to the *logos*, which speaks through him, and can be heard by those with ears to hear. The concept of *logos* harks back to the *apeiron* of Anaximander, and forward to the Absolute or Spirit of Hegel. From our current perspective we could argue that Heraclitus was a kind of pre-existentialist of the Heideggerian kind. It was Heraclitus who first described time as a river into which one can never enter twice at the same place. Indeed, much of Heidegger's thinking is an attempt to continue ancient Greek thought, rather than trade barbs with his contemporaries on the interpretation of Immanuel Kant or Hegel in early twentieth-century German philosophy. In the winter semester of 1966–7 at the University of Freiburg, Heidegger and Eugen Fink (1905–75) conducted a seminar on Heraclitus, finding common themes of life, death and being, and relating it all to Hegel.

[Heidegger] wanted to rejoin the Greeks through the Germans, at the worst moment in their history: is there anything worse, said Nietzsche, than to find oneself facing a German when one was expecting a Greek?

Gilles Deleuze and Félix Guattari, *What Is Philosophy?* (trans. Hugh Tomlinson and Graham Burchell, 1996)

Heraclitus' politics and ethics foreshadowed Christ's exhortation to 'Render therefore unto Caesar the things that are Caesar's; and unto God the things that are God's' (Matthew 22:21) in that he distinguished two types of obedience: that which is given to the *logos*, and that which is given to the one leader of a country. Heraclitus' concept of the *logos* would find its ultimate development in the New Testament Gospel of John (where *logos* is translated as *word*): 'In the beginning was the Word, and the Word was with God, and the Word was God' (John 1:1). John uses the Word to refer not only to God in the sense of a supreme being in heaven, but also to Jesus Christ: 'And the Word was made flesh, and dwelt among us' (John 1:14). Unlike the Christians, Heraclitus did not believe in an afterlife. He identified human existence as taking place in a world of constant flux, in which one was required to make one's own destiny.

'It is impossible to go into the same river twice,' said Heraclitus; no more can you grasp mortal being twice, so as to hold it. So sharp and so swift its change; it scatters and brings together again, nay not again, no nor afterwards; even while it is being formed it fails, it approaches, and it is gone. Hence becoming never ends in being, for the process never leaves off, or is stayed.

Plutarch (*c*.AD 46–120), *On the E at Delphi* (trans. A. O. Prickard, 1918)

Parmenides: philosophy as poetry

One of the chief arguments between contemporary philosophers of the analytic and continental camps involves the charge levelled by analytics that continentals practise forms of philosophy that aren't really philosophy. They are said to be practising 'literary criticism' under cover of philosophy. The French post-structuralist Jacques Derrida (1930–2004) was the main target of this accusation. Continentals are also charged with reading philosophers who aren't really philosophers at all, but are rather writers of 'literature' – Friedrich Nietzsche (1844–1900) stands thus accused. However, the practice of literature and philosophy was, from the beginning, seen as inseparable. The philosopher whom some regard as the greatest of the Presocratics, Parmenides (early fifth century BC), left as his only work a long metaphysical poem divided into two parts, 'The Way of Truth' and 'The Way of Appearance'. In the first poem Parmenides encounters a goddess who shows him two paths: being and not-being. In following the path of being, Parmenides argues that *being* is all there is; there can be no such thing as *not-being*. He sets the tone for much of the metaphysical argument that would follow for the next 2,500 years by arguing that one cannot formulate an expression with a subject followed by the term 'is not'. Only what *is*, what *exists*, can be imagined, discussed, known. Parmenides then goes in search of what is, defining *being* as homogeneous, unchanging and enduring through space and time. Parmenides' world differs utterly from that of Heraclitus; where Heraclitus found change, Parmenides finds the eternally true and enduring.

> Only one story of the way is still left: that a thing is. On this way there are very many signs: that Being is ungenerated and imperishable, entire, unique, unmoved and perfect.
>
> Parmenides (fifth century BC), 'The Way of Truth'
> (trans. Richard McKirahan, 2009)

The English philosopher Alfred North Whitehead (1861–1947) famously remarked that all of Western philosophy was merely a footnote to Plato; but Wittgenstein's student Elizabeth (G. E. M.) Anscombe (1919–2001) wittily noted that Plato's work was a footnote to Parmenides. However, the line of thought that leads from Parmenides to Plato is not a straight one, and it takes a few important detours.

Zeno, Pythagoras and Democritus: mathematics and metaphysics

Zeno of Elea (*c.*490–*c.*430 BC) was a student of Parmenides and is celebrated for formulating paradoxes intended to prove his master's theory of *immutability*. An example would be the arrow paradox, which states that an arrow cannot move at a place where it *is not*; equally, it cannot move at a place where it *is*. A flying arrow is always where it is, so it is at rest. But if it is at rest, it is also not moving. This kind of riddle exercised Aristotle very much (indeed, Aristotle would call Zeno the father of dialectic), and put pressure on early mathematics to come up with concepts that could account for the apparent conflict of stasis and motion.

> Fate is the endless chain of causation, whereby things are; the reason or formula by which the world goes on.
>
> Zeno of Elea (*c*.490–*c*.430 BC) (trans. Jonathan Barnes, 1987)

Pythagoras (*c*.570–*c*.495 BC) and his followers were concerned with using number to explain the universe. The geometrical theorem which states that in a right-angled triangle the square of the hypotenuse is equal to the sum of the squares of the other two sides is the called the Pythagorean theorem. The Babylonians and others had made use of it, but Pythagoras (or his followers) demonstrated it. One of Pythagoras' most enduring teachings was the concept of *metempsychosis* or reincarnation of the soul (sometimes called transmigration). It is one of Plato's essential ideas; it is also fundamental to a number of Eastern religions, and was key to the thought of the American transcendentalist Ralph Waldo Emerson (1803–82) and the

Indian advocate of passive resistance, Mohandas K. Gandhi (1869–1948).

Another Presocratic idea that has had an enormous impact on thinking right up until the present day is atomism: the idea that the world is composed of indestructible, irreducible building blocks. Atomism was first developed by Leucippus (early fifth century BC) and continued by his student Democritus (*c*.460–*c*.370 BC), who believed that things are composed of atoms, which exist in an infinite void (space). Aristotle would reject Democritus' form of atomism because he thought it lacked a teleological order or sense of direction. Teleology – the notion that things have a purpose, tending towards a perfect (or at least meaningful) end – was important for Plato and Aristotle, and the medieval Christian philosophers. For Christian thinkers, the purpose of things was to have been created by God and to fulfil his divine plan. Christian resistance to Charles Darwin's theory of the origin of species (1859) stemmed from its contradiction of the belief that species exist in accordance with a preordained divine plan.

Democritus said that the atoms had two properties, size and shape, while Epicurus added weight as a third.

Aëtius (*c*.396–454), *Opinions*
(trans. C. C. W. Taylor, 1999)

Socrates, Plato and the Socratic dialogue

Plato claimed not to like the group of philosophers who have come to be known as the Sophists, because he thought they used their philosophical skills solely to win arguments, and to attract paying students who wished to develop their rhetorical skills for profit. (Plato did not charge students who attended his Academy.) The most famous of the Sophists was Protagoras (*c*.490–*c*.420 BC) who, ironically, many scholars credit with creating the style of debate that led Plato to develop the Socratic dialogue.

> . . . he thinks that he knows something which he doesn't know, whereas I am quite conscious of my ignorance.
>
> Socrates, from Plato's *Apology*
>
> (trans. Harrold Tarrant, 1954)

Socrates – Plato's teacher – challenged Athenians' received opinions. As a result, he came to be admired and despised in equal measure. As a young man Socrates was a brave soldier, who fulfilled his duties of citizenship (including political service) honourably. Otherwise, his life was devoted to philosophy, which for him was the active pursuit of knowledge rather than the passive contemplation of problems. Socrates *philosophi{ed*.

Socrates philosophized in the street, at the marketplace, wherever men gathered to converse. His technique was to seize upon a subject of the 'what is?' variety. What is good? What is virtue? What is knowledge? His method was to encourage his interlocutor to say what he thought those things might mean, and then, by a series of cunning questions, get him to admit that he has no idea what they mean after all. If it was any consolation to his partner in dialogue, Socrates himself would usually admit that he did not know the answer either. For many, participating in Socratic dialogue was invigorating, exhilarating, the highest form of activity. For others, however, it meant being embarrassed in public. These people became enemies of Socrates.

Socrates was famous throughout Athens, but doubts soon formed about him. Perhaps he asked too many questions, questioned too hard. Perhaps his questioning instilled too much doubt. He was the subject of Aristophanes' (c.448–c.380 BC) play *The Clouds* (423 BC), which poked fun at the intellectual life of fifth-century BC Athens. Unscrupulous teachers of rhetoric abounded, and though Socrates was not one, he was lumped in with them by Aristophanes, and portrayed as a crazed and godless scientist who twists the minds of the young and impressionable in a school called 'The Thinkery', which is burned down by an angry mob.

In real life Socrates became a martyr to philosophy when he was condemned to death in 399 BC. The charges against him included 'not believing in the gods in which the city believes, and of introducing other new divinities'. He was also accused of 'corrupting the young'. Socrates' pupil Plato immortalizes his master's courage in the face of death in *The Apology of Socrates*. As his friends try to console him in his final hours, Socrates continues to philosophize, talking in particular of the immortality of the soul. He calmly drinks the hemlock that the executioner brings to him, after first discussing with the executioner the protocol of his death.

> . . . the life which is unexamined is not worth living.
>
> Socrates, from Plato's *Apology*
>
> (trans. Benjamin Jowett, 1871)

Plato and the world of forms

Plato's key contribution was to look past sense experience and the material world to identify what he called Forms. Forms are a type of *idea* of things. For example, there is an ideal form of a chair; but any chair we might sit upon is merely a pale and inadequate representation of the ideal Form that exists for chairs. It is the same for qualities and virtues, and the Form of good as conceived by Plato is probably indistinguishable from God.

Plato took from his teacher Socrates the concept of philosophy as an activity, and he couches much of his teaching in the form of Socratic dialogues in which knowledge is gradually revealed through the activity of thinking. Plato's epistemology (or theory of knowledge and how we acquire it) is best demonstrated in the *Meno*. What begins as a dialogue concerning the nature of virtue between Socrates and Meno – a follower of the Sophist Gorgias – becomes a demonstration of Plato's theory of knowledge as *remembering* or a 'loss of forgetfulness', a literal translation of the Greek term *anamnesis*. Plato argues that just as there are ideal Forms behind the world of shadows we inhabit, so knowledge already resides in the soul of man, if only he could remember it. Plato's Socrates chooses one of Meno's slaves at random and – in a cunning presentation of the geometry of squares – he gets the slave to appear to remember knowledge about the subject he originally possessed, but had forgotten.

> The soul, then, as being immortal, and having been born again many times, and having seen all things that exist, whether in this world or in the world below, has knowledge of them all.
>
> Plato, *Meno* (trans. Benjamin Jowett, 1871)

Along with the Forms, Plato's other great contribution to philosophy was his elaboration of Pythagoras' idea of the immortality of the soul. Plato was a dualist, which is to say he believed that body and soul are separate entities. In the *Meno* he offers a proof for the immortality of the soul by suggesting that the immortal soul that resides in the body of Meno's slave is the source of his recovered knowledge of geometry. Dualism would be reintroduced into Christian philosophy in the seventeenth century by the French philosopher René Descartes (1596–1650).

Plato's *Republic*: the roots of totalitarianism?

The second half of the twentieth century saw a resurgence of interest in Plato's political thought as expressed in the *Republic* (*c*.380 BC). This was largely because Karl Popper (1902–94), an Austrian philosopher who fled the Nazis and became a British subject, declared Plato an enemy of democracy in his landmark work *The Open Society and Its Enemies* (2 vols, 1945, 1962). In a wide-ranging critique of theories of teleological historicism, Popper brackets Plato with Hegel and Karl Marx (1818–83) as the fathers of totalitarian ideology. (The first volume of his book is subtitled 'The Spell of Plato'.) Of Plato he wrote that the 'anti-equalitarian interpretation of justice in the *Republic* was an innovation, and that Plato attempted to present his totalitarian class rule as "just" while people generally meant by "justice" the exact opposite'. In the aftermath of the Nazi dictatorship of 1933–45, the rise of Josef Stalin (1878–1953) in the Soviet Union, and of

Mao Zedong (1893–1976) in China, the historical roots of total-itarianism came under closer scrutiny. The first comprehensive treatment of the subject was by Hannah Arendt (1906–75) in *The Origins of Totalitarianism* (1951).

Of the five types of government Plato recognized, democracy ranked fourth, just ahead of tyranny. In front of these were aris-tocracy (rule of the 'best'), timocracy (rule by the 'honourable'), and oligarchy (rule by the wealthy). Plato viewed democracy as rule by the masses, whom he considered unfit for the task. He defined tyranny as the rule of a single man who may begin with the people's interests in mind, but soon puts his own interests before theirs.

Plato's republic contained three classes of person: the philoso-pher-kings; the guardians; and the workers and merchants. The philosopher-kings are a very small group who have reached the highest level of philosophical training. The guardians are the management class, who comprise both soldiers and administra-tors; they are, in effect, the government. The workers and merchants, in Plato's ideal world, are marked by the virtue of temperance.

Education is central to Plato's ideal state, and a guardian would receive a thorough education in philosophy, along with physical training. After a period of practical employment a guardian would receive further philosophical instruction. Plato believed that the age of philosophical maturity was fifty, after which a person achieved their full value to themselves and the state.

The social organization of the guardians was also crucial to Plato's republic. It was essentially communist in nature, in that there was very limited private property. Plato went further than most communists in requiring that children be held in common; they were not to know who their parents were. Children would be conceived as the result of breeding festivals in which lots were drawn to pair men and women for breeding on eugenic grounds (that is to say, matches that a committee thought would be most likely to produce *well-born* children). The unions would last only for the duration of the festival. As well as supporting a eugenic programme designed to encourage breeding from the fit, Plato advocated infanticide for 'unfit' children, and for those born to women over the age of forty.

> . . . marriage, the having of wives, and the procreation of children must be governed as far as possible by the old proverb: friends possess everything in common.
>
> Plato, *Republic* (c.380 BC)
> (trans. G. M. A. Grube, 1992)

But Plato, like the leaders of the Soviet Union, believed that women should play an important role in government. (Western democracies would come late to this idea; from the founding of the Soviet Union women were leaders in science and technology.) He described the absurdity of excluding women from government as being akin to preferring long-haired persons over short-haired ones for the task. Some have argued that Plato was a feminist because he separated desire and reproduction from the business of governance. So, along with 'proto-totalitarian' some would add 'proto-feminist' to the new labels that Plato's commentators have applied to him 2,500 years after his death!

The dominant theme of the *Republic* is the role that an understanding of the Forms, of Good, and of mathematics plays in the formation of political leaders. If we bracket out the social blueprint aspect of the *Republic*, it emerges as a text on the importance of education. The most famous scene in the *Republic*, known as 'the allegory of the cave', likens the situation of most people to that of being chained against a wall in a cave. Their only experience of the world is the shadows thrown against the cave walls by things passing in front of a fire; they never directly perceive the world. The philosopher is the person who manages to escape his chains, leave the cave and discover the Forms.

Aristotle: Plato's most famous pupil

As Socrates passed his knowledge to Plato, who acknowledged his master and moved beyond him, so Aristotle, who spent twenty years as Plato's student, surpassed his master, and went on to become tutor to the young Alexander the Great (356–323 BC). Aristotle created the first total system of philosophy, his work setting the example (and the bar) for other great builders of philosophical systems of the future, like Kant and Hegel.

Aristotle's system is built on the idea that philosophy falls into distinct disciplines, each having a different method and requirements for proof. For him these included logic, natural philosophy, metaphysics, philosophy of mind, ethics, political philosophy and aesthetics.

Aristotle created the first system of deductive logic in his *Prior Analytics* with the invention of the *syllogism*. This is a logical argument in which a conclusion is inferred from two premises. A basic example of a syllogism would contain a major premise such as 'All men are mortal'. The minor premise would be 'Socrates is a man'. Therefore, we can deduce the conclusion that 'Socrates is mortal'. Syllogistic logic can be a tricky business, as syllogisms can be valid without being true. For instance, the syllogism 'all men are immortal, Socrates is a man, therefore Socrates is immortal' is just as valid, because it follows syllogistic form; but

34

it is untrue since the first premise is untrue. In another example, 'all men are mortal, Socrates is a philosopher, therefore Socrates is mortal' is a true conclusion, but it is built on an invalid syllogistic form. Aristotle's understanding of logic also includes the philosophy of language, a forerunner of much of contemporary analytic philosophy. Aristotle's teaching of logic would prevail until the early part of the twentieth century, when Gottlob Frege (1848–1925) would create a new system and describe its relation to language. Frege's work would be recognized by Bertrand Russell (1872–1970), giving rise to analytic philosophy.

Aristotle's natural philosophy includes studies in physics, cosmology and, especially, biology. In his *Physics* he explores the nature of form and matter, and cause and effect. He posits the idea of the *unmoved mover*: that which is behind all movement in our universe. This became the argument of *first cause*, used by the medieval Scholastic philosophers to describe God as creator of the universe.

Aristotle's biological works are doubly important because they (a) outline a method, and (b) constitute a programme of research that bears results. His method was to categorize things according to substance, species and genus. This not only provided the means to catalogue plants and animals in a coherent way, it also implied a teleological character in nature, along with a hierarchy that linked man with some notion of the absolute (or God) above him, and lesser beings beneath him. This was the idea of the Great Chain of Being, which placed God at the top, followed (in the later Christian tradition) by various ranks of angels, then man, woman, animals, plants, inorganic matter and, finally, chaos.

Metaphysics: the study of being

Aristotle established metaphysics as 'the study of being *qua* being'. That apparently simple declaration – *Aristotle established metaphysics as 'the study of being* qua *being'* – is one which most historians would agree to be true. But if one asks philosophers to say what it means, disagreement immediately breaks out, leading to many different explanations. What is meant by *metaphysics* would be the first point of contention, irrespective of what Aristotle said; the other term in the sentence to cause broad disagreement is *being*.

Aristotle never used the term metaphysics. Throughout the history of thought, metaphysics has been regarded as the most highfalutin branch of philosophy. One thinks of the extremely difficult technical language employed by Hegel, as opposed to the self-consciously clear presentation of an analytic philosopher like A. J. Ayer, who did not believe in metaphysics. But the origin of the term metaphysics is quite modest. It came about when Andronicus, the first-century BC cataloguer of Aristotle's work, had to place the great philosopher's writings in what he thought to be the correct chronological order. The book we know as the *Metaphysics* is the one that Andronicus placed *after* the *Physics*. Since the prefix *meta* signifies 'after' in Greek, the *Metaphysics* got its name by coming after the *Physics*. (Perhaps there is a warning here for philosophers who want to make things more difficult than they are.)

As for *being*, we might think it an easily definable term; but if this were so, philosophers would be out of a job. In the twentieth century questions of being tended to fall within the scope of such continental philosophers as Martin Heidegger and the Frenchman Jean-Paul Sartre, the former's *Being and Time* (1927) and the latter's *Being and Nothingness* (1943) setting the agenda for existentialism. Analytic philosophers like A. J. Ayer would argue that the work of Heidegger and Sartre consists of little more than abuses of the verb 'to be', and has nothing to do with what Aristotle meant by being. Ayer argued that metaphysics – particularly the metaphysics of Heidegger – was, literally, nonsense. It simply had no meaning.

All men by nature desire to know.

Aristotle, *Metaphysics* (trans. Richard McKeon, 1941)

The whole question of what is meant by being could be viewed as the first question of philosophy. '"Why are there beings at all

instead of nothing?" – this is obviously the first of all questions.'
So declared Heidegger in his *Introduction to Metaphysics* (1935,
published 1953). If being is defined as what *is*, as opposed to what
is not, it is still a difficult concept to grasp. For Aristotle, to inquire
into being was to explore the concept of *substance*. It was a search
for the irreducible.

After Plato's death, Aristotle rejected the notion of Forms and
focused instead on substance, which contains *essence* or that which
does not change. He described substance as a unity of matter and
form; and *divine substance* as substance without matter. Rejecting
the anthropomorphic gods of Olympus, Aristotle believed that
divinity was to be found in the ordered workings of the universe.
Even today – perhaps especially today – it is difficult to find a
generally agreed upon definition of metaphysics among contemporary philosophers. (Professional philosophers tend to be very
cautious people.)

Greek philosophy after Aristotle

Both Plato and Aristotle would undergo numerous interpretations
and reinterpretations over the centuries, as thinkers in each
succeeding era found new relevance in their ideas (or attempted
to make them conform to their own). However, while Plato and
Aristotle dominate Western thought, other ancient Greek thinkers

developed modes of thought that would endure and influence Roman philosophy.

Cynicism, founded by Socrates' friend Antisthenes (*c*.445–*c*.365 BC), holds that true happiness lies in right and intelligent living. Its followers mastered their desires and wants, paring life down to its essentials (as would the nineteenth-century American Transcendentalist Ralph Waldo Emerson).

Scepticism was another major philosophical stance in ancient Greece. While the sceptical attitude may be said to describe philosophers in general, it originally refers to two very different schools of thought. *Pyrrhonian scepticism* originates with Pyrrho (*c*.360–*c*.270 BC). It is a radical approach to thinking that refuses assent to any non-evident proposition; even the 'truths' elicited by sensory perception or the use of reason were judged to be unreliable. This led to a philosophical position in which all judgement was suspended. This state of affairs is referred to by the Greek term *epoché*. (In the early twentieth century Edmund Husserl, the founder of phenomenology, would resurrect the notion of the *epoché* as the goal of his method, known as the transcendental reduction.) *Academic scepticism* was developed by Arcesilaus (316/15–241/0 BC) who was the sixth successor to Plato as head of the Academy. Like Pyrrho, Arcesilaus thought that knowledge of things was impossible; however, he did think that there were degrees of probability, and this difference from Pyrrhonian scepticism allowed the thinker to *act*. Academic scepticism was further developed by the Roman thinker Cicero (106–43 BC).

In contrast to Scepticism was Stoicism, a school of thought associated with Zeno of Citium (*c*.334–*c*.262 BC). Rather than rejecting the evidence upon which knowledge could be based, Stoics erected criteria by which a perception could be treated as knowledge. Is it clear? Can a number of persons agree that it is so? Is it probable? Is it amenable to being incorporated in a system of knowledge? Stoicism remained an influential approach in Roman philosophy, and its proponents included Seneca the Younger (*c*.4 BC–AD 65) and the emperor Marcus Aurelius (AD 121–80).

Epicurus (341–270 BC) further developed the atomistic thought of Democritus in founding his eponymous school of Epicureanism. The goal of Epicureanism was to overcome superstition and belief in gods and divine intervention. Epicureans thought that a scientific understanding of nature, combined with control of bodily desires, would lead to tranquillity, freedom from fear and relief from bodily pain.

Eclecticism is also an important part of the Greek legacy. By its very nature – the idea of building a philosophy taking parts from various schools of thought – it cannot be ascribed to one founder. Prominent eclectics included Panaetius of Rhodes (*c*.185–*c*.110/09 BC), Posidonius of Apameia (*c*.135–51 BC), Philo of Larissa (154/3–84/3 BC) and the Roman Cicero.

Philosophy and religion in the Graeco-Roman world

Greece succumbed to the growing power of the Roman republic following the defeat of the Achaean League at the Battle of Corinth in 146 BC. Sixty years later, in 86 BC, the Athenian Academy itself was destroyed by the troops of the Roman general Lucius Cornelius Sulla. (According to the Romanized Greek historian Plutarch [first century BC], 'he laid hands upon the sacred groves and ravaged the academy'.) But long before these indignities were visited on philosophy's birthplace, the geographical reach of ancient Greek thought had been broadened by the conquests of Alexander the Great in the Near East, North Africa and Asia in the late fourth century BC. Thus the many schools of thought that subsequently flourished in the Mediterranean and Hellenistic worlds continued to bear the philosophical imprint of their classical Greek forebears.

For the educated elites of the increasingly Roman-dominated Mediterranean and Near East of the first century BC and after, Greek-born philosophies such as Stoicism and Epicureanism offered an attractive alternative to traditional polytheistic religion. At the same time, an emerging group of religious cults of a new and very different character were making their presence felt across the Graeco-Roman world. Typified by the mystery cults of Isis,

Cybele and Atargatis, these religions were open to initiates only, and offered their devotees more in the way of private consolation than the traditional gods.

Over the centuries of late Antiquity, however, the old pagan gods, the new mystery cults and the claimed divinity of successive Roman emperors (from 27 BC the first Roman emperor Augustus [63 BC–AD 14] promoted a cult of emperor-worship as a means of moulding his multinational subjects into loyal Roman citizens) would slowly but surely yield to a religion centred on a first-century AD Jewish teacher and miracle-worker from Galilee in Roman-ruled Palestine. That religion would not only conquer the Roman Empire by the fourth century AD, it would also hold sway over Western thought for more than a millennium.

> The various modes of worship, which prevailed in the Roman world, were all considered by the people, as equally true; by the philosopher, as equally false; and by the magistrate, as equally useful.
>
> Edward Gibbon, *The History of the Decline and Fall of the Roman Empire* (1776–88)

PART TWO

Christianity Triumphant

1st century to 16th century

Judaism was the first monotheistic belief system, and it traces its history back to the early part of the second millennium BC, some 1,500 years before the rise of philosophy in ancient Greece. In common with Christianity and Islam, Judaism is an Abrahamic religion – that is to say, it derives from Abraham, patriarch of the Israelites. Islam regards Abraham as a prophet. Muhammad (c.570/1–632) is a descendant of Abraham via his son Ishmael.

Judaism is a unified tradition of religious belief, social custom and law. It is codified in written texts, the first of which is the Torah (or Pentateuch). These are the five books of Moses which correspond to the first five books of the Old Testament of the Christian Bible: Genesis, Exodus, Leviticus, Numbers and Deuteronomy. These texts are important because theology – a cornerstone of Western thought – begins with their study.

Interpretation of Talmudic texts also leads to the first practice of *hermeneutics* from around 515 BC. Hermeneutics is the interpretation of written texts that began with Talmudic and biblical scholarship and was developed by nineteenth-century German philosophers to include critical strategies for understanding texts (not only written ones, but 'texts' such as social practice).

A new kind of God

The Jewish God differs from the ancient Greek and Roman gods in that He cares about humankind. (Greek deities could show concern for humans, but not as much as they had for themselves.) In a time and a place that could be harsh and unrelenting, the God of the Jews offered something unique: He anointed the Jews as His chosen people, and rescued them from slavery in Egypt through the leadership of His prophet, Moses.

While the Jewish God cares about His people, their relationship with Him is fearful. They dare not speak His name. When Moses asks God what His name is, God replies 'I am that I am' (Yahweh, variously translated as 'I am who I am', 'I am what I am'). Even today, many Jews write his name as 'G-d', following the ancient rule against using his name. By contrast, the Christian God is more approachable, and Christian ritual urges the faithful to praise his name in song and prayer.

The core beliefs of Judaism were codified by the medieval Jewish scholar and physician Maimonides (1135–1204), known as RaMBaM in Hebrew literature. His thirteen articles of faith were:

1. God exists
2. God is one and unique
3. God is incorporeal
4. God is eternal
5. Prayer is to God only
6. The prophets spoke truth
7. Moses was the greatest of the prophets
8. The Written and Oral Torah were given to Moses
9. There will be no other Torah
10. God knows the thoughts and deeds of men
11. God will reward the good and punish the wicked
12. The Messiah will come
13. The dead will be resurrected

The Jewish God not only gave people hope during their natural lifetimes, but he also offered the opportunity of eternal life in the resurrection of the dead. He guided ethical thinking and behaviour by rewarding the good and punishing the wicked. Of course, the definition of good had been one of the key problems in Platonic thought; and Maimonides' first four articles of faith raise a series of new philosophical issues for which an Aristotelian training would prove useful. God exists; what *is* God? God is one and unique; what is *divine substance*? God is incorporeal; what is the nature of a non-embodied being? God is eternal; what is eternity? What is time?

Christianity: God becomes man

Christianity took the personal God of Judaism and made him incarnate as a man, Jesus Christ (*c.*5 BC–*c.*AD 30), living among ordinary people in Palestine. Christ's life, teachings and crucifixion are described in the four Gospels in the New Testament of the Christian Bible (written *c.*AD 70–100). His followers believed that he was the son of God, the redeemer or Messiah foretold in prophecy. His reputation as a charismatic teacher and as a healer and miracle-worker was widespread. He attracted crowds numbering in the thousands (which translates as hundreds of thousands by today's standards, when measured as a percentage of the population).

Jesus was seen as a threat to the authority of the Sanhedrin or Jewish Council, which condemned him for refusing to deny that he was the son of God. The Jewish elders brought Jesus to Pontius Pilate, prefect of the Roman province of Judaea, and demanded his execution. Pilate did not consider Jesus to be a threat, but agreed to his crucifixion when Jewish leaders reminded him that Jesus' claim to be king of the Jews was a challenge to Roman authority. Pilate famously washed his hands of the matter, thereby sealing the fate of Jesus as a martyr. The followers of Jesus, who witnessed his healing and teaching, thought that they were seeing God Himself in action – a belief confirmed when, three days after the Crucifixion, Jesus was reported to have risen from the dead, appearing to several of his disciples before ascending into heaven.

The Jews do not recognize Jesus as God, or even as a prophet. Islam regards Jesus as a messenger of God sent to lead the Israelites. But for Christians Jesus is the only God. According to Catholic dogma, Jesus anointed his disciple Peter to lead one holy, catholic and apostolic church, whose beliefs were codified at the Council of Nicaea in 325. Christ's post-resurrection command to found a new church led to a great missionary movement that would spread Christian teaching beyond the boundaries of the Roman Empire. By the end of the fourth century, Christianity had become the state religion of the Roman Empire. The appeal of Christian teaching – redemption of sins and eternal life after death – overturned pagan beliefs and created a new worldview that placed man at the centre of religious belief and practice.

The spread of Christianity

Probably the most influential of the early Christian missionaries was Paul of Tarsus (*c*.AD 5–*c*.67). Having experienced a famous conversion on the road to Damascus, he became a prominent apostle of Christianity, helping to spread its gospel across the Roman Empire and making a critical contribution to the development of Christian belief. It was largely down to the influence of Paul (whose writings constitute a significant portion of the New Testament) that the cult of Jesus was transformed into a universal religion.

> There is neither Jew nor Greek, there is neither bond nor free, there is neither male nor female: for ye are all one in Christ Jesus.
>
> The Epistle of Paul to the Galatians (3:28)

Christianity's rise from an underground movement to state religion of the Roman Empire is a story of bloody persecution. Of Jesus' eleven remaining apostles after his crucifixion (Judas Iscariot committed suicide after betraying Jesus), ten were killed for their beliefs; only John the Apostle (*c*.AD 6–*c*.100) died a natural death, after being banished to the island of Patmos. What began as sporadic persecution of Christians became official state policy under the emperor Nero (*c*.AD 37–68). In AD 64 a fire that burned for five and a half days and destroyed a sizable portion of Rome was blamed on the Christians (Nero himself was suspected of starting the blaze).

> . . . an immense multitude was convicted, not so much of the crime of firing the city, as of hatred against mankind. Mockery of every sort was added to their deaths. Covered with the skins of beasts, they were torn by dogs and perished, or were nailed to crosses, or were doomed to the flames and burnt, to serve as a nightly illumination, when daylight had expired.
>
> Tacitus (c.AD 56–c.120), *Annals* XV.44 (trans. Alfred John Church and William Jackson Brodribb, 1942)

After this, mob persecution of Christians became a regular event; when they refused to recant their beliefs and worship the gods of Rome, they were put to death. This led to widespread martyrdom, which had the effect of increasing Christianity's popularity. While it may seem odd from a modern perspective, their belief in an afterlife that promised heaven led many early Christians to welcome an early death as preferable to their miserable existence on earth (what today we would call their low socio-economic status). It was not uncommon for groups of Christians to goad the Roman authorities into killing them. The Roman consul Arrius Antonius (c.AD 37–119) obliged several Christians when they demanded to be executed, but sent the rest of the crowd away, suggesting there was plenty of rope and an abundance of cliffs available for those who wished to commit suicide. Arrius sensed the danger in being used as an instrument by Christians seeking martyrdom, forcing the state into public killings which, eventually, would undermine its rule.

Christian belief

The key idea in Christianity is that Christ was made incarnate by God and placed on earth to redeem humankind's sins through his crucifixion. Christians believe that Jesus died for our sins. (Christ is often portrayed as the lamb of God going to the slaughter, and Protestant sects talk of being 'washed in the blood' of Christ when one's sins are forgiven.) By believing in Christ and through the sacrament of confession, man can repent for his sins and gain eternal life. The Church instituted seven sacraments which establish rituals that bear upon every aspect of life from birth (baptism) to death (extreme unction). The other sacraments are confirmation, the Eucharist (Holy Communion), penance (confession), holy orders (ordination to the priesthood) and matrimony (marriage). The Eucharist is at the centre of the Catholic rite. In a ritual which echoes that of the Last Supper (when Christ ate a meal with his apostles prior to his arrest) the priest offers, as a sacrifice to God, bread and wine. Catholics believe that the bread and wine are the actual flesh and blood of Christ, of which they partake. The phenomenon that occurs during the course of the Mass which transforms bread and wine into flesh and blood is known as *transubstantiation*.

Christianity promises eternal life to those who follow it (and eternal damnation to those who violate its laws). The sins that could lead to damnation are more or less the same as those codified in the Ten Commandments, which God handed to Moses. They establish God as having dominion over everything, and proscribe the use of his name in vain, as well as murder, adultery, theft, false witness and covetousness (of a neighbour's wife or possessions). The faithful are exhorted to honour the Sabbath and their parents. Crimes such as murder and theft had been proscribed by civil law for millennia, and had punishments attached to them, ranging from imprisonment to banishment to execution. The Church made punishment for the gravest sins eternal. The commission of a *mortal* sin (as opposed to a minor, venial one) without confession meant burning in hell for eternity.

But the fearful, and unbelieving, and the abominable, and murderers, and whoremongers, and sorcerers, and idolaters, and all liars, shall have their part in the lake which burneth with fire and brimstone: which is the second death.

Book of the Revelation of Saint John the Divine (21:8)

Greek philosophy's last gasp

During the period of Roman persecution of Christians two schools of philosophy that began in ancient Greece continued to flourish: Stoicism and Scepticism. Stoicism, which began around 300 BC with Zeno of Citium, enjoyed currency through the reign of the emperor Marcus Aurelius. Scepticism started with the work of Pyrrho of Elis in the fourth century BC and was developed by Sextus Empiricus (c.AD 200).

The endurance of the terms 'stoical' and 'sceptical' in the twenty-first-century English lexicon are a testimony to how influential these schools were during the Roman period. Today, if someone is stoical we mean they face the slings and arrows of misfortune with a calm demeanour. If we say someone is sceptical we mean they are not likely to believe an explanation that is being offered them vis-à-vis anything from the existence of God to the condition of a used car. While these lingering traces of the ancient concepts are partially accurate, they do not do justice to the sophisticated and systematic thought that lies behind them.

For the Stoics this world is the best of all possible worlds. It is divinely ordered and the job of persons with free will is to find their place in it. The concept of the best of all possible worlds would be elaborated by the German Gottfried Wilhelm Leibniz (1646–1716). The Stoics focus on the concept of *free will* versus *determinism.* Free will is a state of affairs in which a person chooses his actions freely; that is to say, his choice is not determined by some outside force. Determinism is the doctrine that every event has a cause. This view is at odds with the notion of free will, but is of enormous use in science, where events need to have causes in order to be understood. The concept of free will would be central to the thought of the Church Fathers in the medieval period, because it is necessary to the concepts of sin and grace. One must freely choose right or good to achieve grace. Sin, on the other hand, represents the choice to do wrong or evil.

The Sceptics were, well, sceptical of Stoicism. A sceptical tendency had always existed in Greek philosophy, and it was continued by Pyrrho who, though he left no writings, was responsible for a legacy that, at its extreme, advocated the total distrust of the senses, and in a more moderate form counselled against unnecessary speculation.

[Zeno] simply considered a real scientific knowledge of things to be altogether impossible. His fundamental principle was, that there is nothing true or false, right or wrong, honest or dishonest, just or unjust; that there is no standard in anything, but that all things depend upon law and custom, and that uncertainty and doubt belong to everything.

John McClintock and James Strong, *Cyclopaedia of Biblical, Theological and Ecclesiastical Literature* (1885)

An original development in Hellenistic philosophy arose in the third century in the form of Neoplatonism. Developed by Plotinus (c.AD 204/5–70), Neoplatonism takes a mystical view of Plato and in most cases tries to combine his ideas with the new ideas of Christianity. One of the most prominent Neoplatonists was Julian the Apostate (AD 331/2–63), who was the last non-Christian emperor of Rome. Julian was truly, in the Platonic sense, a philosopher-king. He resisted the influence of Christianity, fearing it would cause the dissolution of the empire. Julian's view is vindicated by the eighteenth-century British historian Edward Gibbon (1737–94), whose *The History of the Decline and Fall of the Roman Empire* (1776–88) argued that Christianity's focus on a world to come distracted citizens from their duty of active participation in the social present, and that the 'weakness' of Christianity helped bring about the decline of Roman culture by eroding its martial virtue. Julian thought that the way to avoid the dissolution of the Roman Empire was a return to ancient values. As a philosopher he emphasized the importance of the ancient gods for their allegorical teachings, while adopting aspects of Platonic thought.

Julian, the Stoics and the Sceptics represent the last gasps of pre-Christian philosophy. Now, for more than a millennium, Christianity would maintain strict control over the development of thought in the West.

The dominance of Christian thought

After his victory at the Battle of the Milvian Bridge (312), Constantine the Great (*c.* 272–337) became the sole ruler of the Roman Empire. Constantine is said to have converted to Christianity after experiencing a vision in which God assured his troops of victory if they marked their shields with the Christian cross. Despite Constantine's triumph, the decline of the Western Roman Empire was already under way. Christianity would continue, however. Odoacer, the *foederatus* (or tribal ally of Rome) who ousted the last Western emperor Romulus Augustus (*c.*461/3– before 488) to become king of Italy in 476, was of Germanic descent and, most importantly, a Christian. As the Roman Empire in the West fragmented, powerful tribal groups such as the Franks and the Visigoths continued the practice of Christianity in the successor states they established in Western Europe. The survival of the Eastern Roman (or Byzantine) Empire after the fall of the Western Empire assured the vigorous transmission of Christian thought and practice in the East, though the Muslim Arab conquest of Syria, Palestine and North Africa would dim the flame of Near Eastern Christianity in the seventh century. The early eighth century brought further Islamic penetration of Christendom as the armies of the Umayyad caliphate crossed the

Strait of Gibraltar (711) and conquered the Visigothic kingdom of Hispania (modern Spain).

The next Christian emperor to rule in Western Europe was the Frankish king Charlemagne (*c.*742–814), who expanded his territories into an empire that covered much of Western and Central Europe. Charlemagne was crowned Imperator Romanum by Pope Leo I on Christmas Day 800, and presided over the so-called Carolingian Renaissance, the first renewal of learning in the West during the medieval period.

Christianity was prone to internal division from the outset. The church councils of Nicaea (325) and Constantinople (381) repudiated the Arian form of Christianity, which differed from mainstream Christological doctrine in its teachings concerning the relationship of the three entities of the Trinity (that is, the three coexisting divine persons – Father, Son and Holy Spirit – which Christians consider to be a fundamental attribute of God). Further significant splits in the Church followed the councils of Ephesus (431) and Chalcedon (451). But Christianity's principal fault line was the gradual souring of the relationship between the Western and Eastern churches over the centuries due to ecclesiastical and theological differences, culminating in a formal schism in 1054 between the Roman Catholic and Orthodox churches.

The flourishing of Christianity was good news for Latin as a *lingua franca* because it became not only the official language of the Roman Empire, but also of the Western Church. This, however, was bad news for philosophy in the sense that the Romans eventually lost their facility for the Greek language; as a consequence, knowledge of Greek thought declined to the point where it, too, was almost entirely lost to the West. (Some knowledge of Greek *was* preserved in the work of early medieval Irish scholars. Johannes Scotus Eriugena [*c*.810–*c*.877], for instance, who worked at the Frankish court of Charles the Bald [823–877], was a master of Greek, translating the writings of the Neoplatonist theologian Pseudo-Dionysius [late fifth–early sixth century] from that language into Latin.)

Another factor that initially worked against Greek philosophy was Church teaching. The Church now became the most powerful force for the expression of ideas. It had teachers (priests) and students (congregations) in enormous numbers. Churches effectively replaced the Academy as places of learning. Compared to the deep inquiries of Democritus, Plato and Aristotle, what the Church had to offer was dogma rather than unfettered philosophical inquiry. God was the source of all things: that was to be the beginning and end of all thought. This necessarily limited the scope of a philosopher's work. Faith, not knowledge, became the ruling paradigm. The challenge for Christian philosophers would be how to introduce philosophical inquiry inside a worldview that presupposed certain conclusions and was quick to punish those who departed from them.

One of the means by which the Church assumed the mantle of teacher and disseminator of ideas was the development of monastic communities. The monks who lived in these communities were organized into orders created by spiritual leaders – the first Western order of monks was founded by St Benedict of Nursia (480–547), who laid down strict rules of work and prayer that govern most monastic orders. In one sense, monasteries were proto-universities. Prospective members of a religious order (novices) would be taught grammar, logic and rhetoric, to which would later be added mathematics, music and astronomy. Monasteries were not only centres of teaching and learning, they were also among the most important libraries in the history of Western thought. As literacy declined for nearly three centuries in Europe, beginning in the fourth century, monasteries gained importance as places where texts were both copied and stored.

Augustine of Hippo: theology and philosophy

The development of Christian theology as a philosophical practice begins with St Augustine of Hippo (354–430), who is to be credited with a number of firsts. While his place in the pantheon of philosophers is assured, he is no less significant for having published the first autobiography. Augustine's *Confessions* (397–8) is important not only because it contains a vital account of spiritual and intellectual conversion to Christianity, but also because it is the first text in which the first-person singular voice, the *I*, comes into play in this form in Western thought. This is critical not only because of its place in the history of genre writing, but because it represents a new attempt to find a human rather than divine ground for knowledge. The *Confessions* laid the ground for Descartes' *Discourse on Method* (1637) more than a thousand years later, in which Descartes formulated his famous declaration *cogito ergo sum*: 'I think therefore I am', signalling the arrival of the human subject at the centre of the world, rather than occupying the peripheral, passive position of being acted upon.

> I intend to remind myself of my past foulness and carnal corruptions, not because I love them but so that I may love you, my God. It is from love of your love that I make the act of recollection. The recalling of my wicked ways is bitter in my memory, but I do it so that you may be sweet to me, a sweetness touched by no deception, a sweetness serene and content.
>
> St Augustine of Hippo, *Confessions* (397–8)
> (trans. Henry Chadwick, 1991)

Augustine helped to define Church orthodoxy negatively by saying what it *wasn't*. The things it wasn't were defined by him as errors, known as heresies or unauthorized modifications of belief. Augustine's identification of heresies has an importance far beyond its relevance for the Church. For instance, in defining the heresy of Pelagianism (named after its proponent, the – probably British-born – ascetic Pelagius [354–420/440]), Augustine prefigured an important ethical principle explored by Kant, that *ought* implies *can*. Pelagianism claims that human nature is not tainted by original sin and that man can freely choose between good and evil without God's help, thereby violating Church teaching that the sacrament of baptism is necessary to cleanse original sin. It was this promoting of the possibility of human perfectibility without God's help that made Pelagianism a heresy.

Augustine's *Confessions* prefigures the modern period not only with its first-person voice, but also with its subject matter. Augustine confesses the sinful ways of his youth, which involved not only fornication but also heresy. In this respect Augustine was well qualified to be the clarifier of Christian doctrine. As a young man he was a follower of the Manichaean heresy – the idea that there is a balance of good and evil in the world that elevates the Devil to parity with God.

Augustine's mature masterpiece is *The City of God* (413–27), which, like the *Confessions*, continues in print to this day. Written as a consolation for Christians after the Visigothic sack of Rome in 410, it elaborates the Christian life as one that is not focused on the present, temporal world, but one which looks forward to eternal life in the city of God or heaven. *The City of God* shows that Augustine had some knowledge of Aristotle and Plato – the latter coming from his reading of the Neoplatonists.

> For to this earthly city belong the enemies against whom I have to defend the city of God.
>
> St Augustine of Hippo, *The City of God* (413–27)
>
> (trans. Marcus Dodds, 1871)

The Neoplatonists represented a continuation of ancient Greek thought that could appeal to Christians and other believers in a monotheistic God. For Plotinus, the movement's founder, whose collected writings on the subject are found in the *Enneads*, the universe is predicated on the *One*, the notion of the transcendental Good borrowed from Plato. The One gives birth to ideas, which Plato called *nous*. Ideas inhabit souls, and some souls come to inhabit bodies, thereby providing humankind with its link to knowledge and the Good.

As Neoplatonism developed it incorporated some of Aristotle's ideas (particularly his logic), and this is evident in the work of Plotinus' pupil Porphyry (234–*c*.305). Neoplatonism wasn't always a comfortable fit with Christianity. Porphyry wrote a fifteen-book treatise *Against the Christians*, in which he derided Christianity as stupid and as a 'confused and vicious sect', and called St Peter a liar. Yet it is probably from Porphyry that Augustine acquired his indirect knowledge of Aristotle.

> And even if Christ's suffering was carried out according to God's plan, even if he was meant to suffer punishment – at least he might have faced his suffering nobly and spoken words of power and wisdom to Pilate, his judge, instead of being made fun of like a peasant boy in the big city.
>
> Porphyry (234–c. 305), *Against the Christians*
> (trans. R. Joseph Hoffmann, 1994)

Augustine was a bold ethicist who insisted – against Plato and the Greek tradition (and much of the ethical philosophy of his day) – that knowing what one *ought* to do does not presuppose that one *actually* (or automatically or necessarily) does it. He argues that God created the world as good, and He did not create evil. Evil arises not from God, but from humankind electing to deviate from the path of righteousness.

Augustine has been the stimulus for much important twentieth-century thinking on love and the concept of empathy, especially among the students of Edmund Husserl (1859–1938), the founder of phenomenology. Love was at the heart of Augustine's concept of the will, as is pithily demonstrated in his teaching: 'Love, and do what you will.' The implication is that by loving one follows the path of righteousness, freely electing to do good and avoid evil. Hannah Arendt's doctoral thesis *Love and St Augustine* (1929) is evidence of the importance with which Augustine was regarded in German universities before 1933, when the Nazis came to power.

The rise of Islam

At the beginning of the seventh century, Christianity faced a challenge from a new monotheistic faith. Islam's adherents submitted themselves to Allah, whom they regarded as the one true God. Around 610 the Arabian Muhammad ibn 'Abdull h (*c*.570/1– 632) received what he believed were revelations from God. Chased out of Mecca, he fled to Medina in 622 (an event known as the Hegira), where he founded an Islamic community. Thereafter Islam spread swiftly throughout the region. After Muhammad's death, Muslim Arabs fought a series of wars of conquest which would disseminate the Islamic faith from its Arabian heartland to Central Asia in the east and Spain in the west. Islam was founded at a time when doctrinal controversies were beginning to fracture the relationship between Greek Orthodox and Roman Christianity. These tensions between the Eastern and Western churches may well have hastened the rise of Islam as a dominant force in the medieval world.

Islam views Muhammad as the last in a line of prophets that began with Abraham and includes Jesus Christ. The holy book of Islam is the Quran, which contains accounts by Muhammad's followers of the word of God as spoken directly to him. In common with Judaism and Christianity, Islam is a monotheistic and Abrahamic religion. In common with Christianity, Islam believes in angels, resurrection of the body, and heaven and hell. By contrast, Islam holds that Jesus was a prophet, but not the son of God. In attesting the oneness of God, Muslims dismiss the Christian idea of the Holy Trinity as a form of polytheism. Muslims follow the Five Pillars of Islam, which involve a testament of belief (the *shahadah*), prayer five times a day (*salah*), fasting during the month of Ramadan (*sawm*), alms-giving (*zakat*) and the pilgrimage to Mecca (*hajj*), which Muslims must make at least once in their lifetime, if they can afford to do so.

Those who disbelieve among the People of the Book and the idolaters will have the Fire of Hell, there to remain. They are the worst of creation.

Those who believe and do good deeds are the best of creation. Their reward with their Lord is everlasting gardens graced with flowing streams, where they will stay forever.

Quran, Sura 98 (trans. M. A. A. Abdel Haleem, 2004)

The role of Islam in the transmission of Greek philosophy

During the period when understanding of the Greek language had largely disappeared from Western Europe, all that was known of Aristotle's work were translations of his *Categories*, *On Interpretation*, *Topics* and *Prior Analytics* by the Roman philosopher Anicius Manlius Severinus Boëthius (*c*.480–524/5), known simply as Boethius. The rest of ancient Greek philosophy is available to us today only because Islamic scholars preserved the texts by translating them into Arabic. Essential to the survival of these translations was the introduction of the codex, the direct ancestor of the modern book, around 360, which would gradually replace the scroll. The Islamic world started producing paper in Baghdad in 794/5 after learning the technique from Chinese prisoners of war. (The Chinese invented paper during the Han Dynasty in the first century AD.) Paper would not be introduced in Europe until around 1150 in Islamic Spain.

The transmission of Greek texts from the Arab to the Western world falls into two stages: the first occurred in Baghdad during the eighth and ninth centuries, when Greek works were translated into Arabic; the second stage took place during the crusading era of the twelfth and thirteenth centuries, as Europeans began the reconquest of territories lost to Islam during the Arab conquests. It was in this period that Western scholars discovered the Arabic translations of the Greek classics and retranslated them into Latin. These Latin texts would eventually be translated into the vernacular languages of Europe.

The first translations of ancient Greek texts into Arabic by Islamic scholars were made under the Abbasid dynasty (750–1258), during which earlier religious objections to Greek thinking were dismissed. Abbasid philosophers argued that it was the duty of Islamic scholars to gather knowledge wherever it might be found. In Baghdad, Caliph Harun al-Rashid (763/6–809) created the House of Wisdom, a library and translation centre where the work of preserving ancient thought was carried out. Translations of Pythagoras, Plato, Aristotle, Hippocrates, Euclid (*fl.*300 BC), Plotinus, and Galen (AD 129–199/217) were made under the direction of his son, Caliph Abdallah-al-Mamun (786–833). The Nestorian* Christian scholar Hunayn ibn Ishaq (809–73) was in overall charge of translation, rendering many texts himself. The most renowned translator of the period was the Sabian† mathematician and astronomer Th bit ibn Qurra (826–901).

The scholars of the House of Wisdom did more than render faithful translations of ancient texts. They were also philosophers

---

* The Nestorian church was a schismatic Christian church condemned as heretical by the councils of Ephesus (431) and Chalcedon (451).

† The Sabians were a monotheistic religious group who followed the fourth book of Abrahamic tradition.

in their own right, combining their knowledge of ancient Greece with the medical and mathematical advances of India to create a locus of intellectual activity that was radical in its thinking and international in character. In addition to his work as a translator, ibn Qurra argued that the earth revolved around the sun, and not vice versa, six centuries before Nicolaus Copernicus (1473–1543). He also determined that the length of time it took the Earth to orbit the Sun is 365 days, six hours, nine minutes and twelve seconds. (Contemporary calculations using computers show he was off by only two seconds.) Work such as ibn Qurra's gave the House of Wisdom an importance in the Islamic world beyond its function as a translation factory. Not only was it a glorious library and philosophers' workshop, it was also a kind of proto-university, and the greatest repository of knowledge the world had ever seen.

In 1258 Mongol forces under the leadership of Hulagu Khan (c.1217–65) destroyed the House of Wisdom. It was a blow from which Islamic culture never fully recovered. After the destruction of the House of Wisdom, the Christian monasteries of Europe would gradually take the place of Islamic centres of learning.

The first universities

The most important development for the spread of ideas, the professionalization of theology (and by implication, philosophy), and the creation of the modern idea of the student, was the university. The first European university was at Bologna and was founded in 1088 (or 1113, depending upon which account one credits). In quick succession universities were founded at Paris (1090) and Oxford (1096). Other European cities soon followed suit: Montpellier (1131), Salamanca (1134), Cambridge (1209) and Coimbra (1290). The universities were incorporated by kingdoms or communes, and staffed by theologians whose purpose was to teach Christian doctrine while at the same time educating pupils in the classical trivium of grammar, logic and rhetoric. After completing the trivium students would take the quadrivium, which included arithmetic, music, geometry and astronomy. This was the first prescription for a liberal arts education. The medieval university required liberal arts candidates to have a broader training in mathematics and the sciences than those of the twentieth and twenty-first centuries.

Clash of Christianity and Islam

Coincidental with the rise of the university was a clash between Christianity and Islam. Efforts to recover Iberia for Christendom had begun shortly after the Islamic conquest of the peninsula in the early eighth century, and in 1095 Pope Urban II (*c*.1042– 99) called for a crusade to wrest the Holy Land from Muslim control. The First Crusade resulted from a request to the papacy from the Byzantine emperor Alexius Comnenos (1048–1118) for help in defending his beleaguered empire against the Seljuk Turks, who had overrun Anatolia following their defeat of the Byzantines at the Battle of Manzikert (1071). Urban II invited all Christians to make war against the Turks. In exchange, crusaders would not only have an opportunity to participate in a great adventure, but they would also be granted immediate remission of their sins. In effect, they were being granted eternal life. It was a win-win situation for Christian warriors: survive and return home covered in glory; or die for Christ and enjoy eternal life. The effect of the Crusades was to create a powerful anti-Islamic (and ultimately anti-Semitic) feeling in Western Europe.

Medieval Islamic culture and Western thought

The return of Islamophobia in the present day colours our view of Islamic philosophy, the study of which had steadily grown in the West during the nineteenth and twentieth centuries prior to the escalation of terrorist acts culminating in the destruction of the Twin Towers in New York City on 11 September 2001. The problem is that ignoring Islamic philosophy gives a fatally imbalanced view of the history of Western thought. The Islamicization of Spain had resulted in a renaissance of philosophical culture when, in the period after Augustine, Western thought was in the doldrums. The scope and majesty of the medieval Islamic world-view can be seen in the Alhambra, the great Moorish palace at Granada in Andalusia, constructed in the mid-fourteenth century. It is a building of remarkable delicacy, integrated into its environment in ways that demonstrate science in the service of architecture, which in turn serves the purposes of worship, rule and study.

The most important Arab thinker at the turn of the first millennium was Ab Al S n, whose latinized name is Avicenna (*c*.980–1037). Avicenna was a physician who wrote extensively on medicine and health issues, as well as being a philosopher who interpreted Aristotle from an Islamic perspective. While he was born in Afshana in present-day Uzbekistan, Avicenna travelled widely in the Arab world, seeking patronage. Changing political fortunes caused him to flee for his life on more than one occasion. His ultimate employment was as physician and scientific adviser to Prince Abu Ja'far 'Ala Addaula (*r*. 1008–1042), ruler of Mesopotamia, Azerbaijan and Armenia, whom he accompanied as physician and general literary and scientific adviser during several military campaigns. One of Avicenna's major contributions to metaphysics was his distinction between *existence* and *essence*. Avicenna identified essence as that which endures unchanged in perpetuity, while existence is contingent or governed by chance.

The Arabic influence on Western philosophy, once again through interpretation of Aristotle, continued with Ibn Rushd, Abu'l Walid Muhammad (1126–98), commonly referred to in the Arab world as Ibn Rushd and in the West as Averroes. Averroes was born in Spain in Córdoba, then the centre of Islamic learning in the West.

> If movement were a change from the substance in which a thing occurs and a displacement of its essence to an opposite substance, then amazingly, the soul would change its substance by its own movement – that is, [it would] displace its actual existence by something opposite to it, thereby destroying itself.
>
> Averroes (1126–98), *Middle Commentary on Aristotle's* De Anima (trans. Alfred L. Ivry, 2002)

In a world dominated by competing religious orthodoxies, Averroes fought the corner for secular inquiry. He held that there were two roads to knowledge: one through religion (revelation), the other through philosophical inquiry (reason). Averroes argued that philosophy and religion held equal places in their search for the same truth. His most enduring work is the provocatively titled

The Incoherence of the Incoherence, which was a response to an argument by the Muslim theologian Al-Ghazali (1058–1111), whose book *The Incoherence of the Philosophers* denounced the views of Avicenna and defended revelation over reason as the way to truth. Averroes' commentaries on Aristotle were inspired by his desire to overcome what he saw as the errors of Neoplatonism. Like Plato, however, he believed that philosophy was the best training for political leaders. He was sceptical of religious leaders.

> The source of their unbelief is in their hearing high-sounding names such as 'Socrates', 'Hippocrates', 'Plato', 'Aristotle' and their likes and the exaggeration and misguid-edness of groups of their followers.
>
> Al-Ghazali (1058–1111), *The Incoherence of the Philosophers*
> (trans. Michael E. Marmura, 1997)

Coincidentally, the leading Jewish philosopher of the period (and perhaps of all time), Moses ben Maimon or Maimonides, was also born in Córdoba and was an exact contemporary of Averroes. Maimonides was a prolific writer across a number of disciplines, including medicine, theology and philosophy. He was a practising physician who wrote his medical texts in Arabic; but his most enduring legacy is his codification of Jewish law in his fourteen-volume *Mishneh Torah*. However, the book for which Maimonides is best known (it is in print today!) is his wonderfully titled *Guide of the Perplexed*, in which he attempts to reconcile religious belief with philosophical thought. The work of Maimonides, along with that of Averroes, paved the way for further elaboration of Aristotelian thought in the work of the greatest of all Church philosophers, Thomas Aquinas (*c.*1225–74).

We are thus like a person whose surroundings are from time to time lit up by lightning, while in the intervals he is plunged into pitch-dark night. Some of us experience such flashes of illumination frequently, until they are in almost perpetual brightness, so that the night turns for them into daylight.

Maimonides (1135–1204), *The Guide of the Perplexed*
(trans. Chaim Rabin, 1995)

The Rise of Scholasticism

The growth of universities and the education of a new class of theologian-philosophers revivified the Church. These writers developed a system of thinking called Scholasticism – a rigorously logical method of defining and defending Christian belief. Ironically, Islamic scholars provided the Church with the means for its further advancement (and the persecution of Muslims) with their translations of Aristotle and commentaries by Avicenna and Averroes. The road from Augustine would culminate in the work of the greatest of the Schoolmen (as the were called), the Italian Dominican theologian and philosopher Thomas Aquinas. His teaching was so complete and so revered that he was given the name *Doctor Angelicus*. But before the perfection of Thomism (as Aquinas's philosophy is called), the way was paved by Peter Abelard's (*c*.1079–1142) work in logic.

> Now the more I was taken up with these pleasures, the less time I could give to philosophy and the less attention I paid to my school. It was utterly boring for me to have to go to the school, and equally wearisome to remain there and to spend my days on study when my nights were sleepless with love-making.
>
> Peter Abelard (*c*. 1079–1142), *Letters of Abelard and Héloïse*
> (trans. Helen Waddell, 1974)

Abelard was a French theologian-philosopher who as a young man produced a masterpiece in the form of his standard text *Logic for Beginners*, published before 1121. His philosophy is mainly devoted to the rational expression of Church teaching. He was also a pioneer in ethics, arguing that human actions should be judged according to the intentions of the subject. The concept of *intentionality*, first raised in Aristotle, would later be developed by Aquinas and incorporated into Edmund Husserl's early twentieth-century phenomenology, and Maurice Merleau-Ponty's (1908–61) theories of perception.

The most enduring popular image of Abelard is as the lover of Héloïse d'Argenteuil (c.1098–1164). Records of Héloïse's origins have been lost, so little is known about her early life except that she came from a humble background. Héloïse had a remarkable intellect. She mastered Latin, Greek and Hebrew texts, and was adept at logic and rhetoric, making her exceptional among women of the day. She was living with her Uncle Fulbert, a canon of Notre Dame Cathedral in Paris, when Abelard became her tutor and they fell passionately in love. They conceived a son, whom she christened Astrolabe, after the scientific instrument for navigating by the stars. They secretly married, and Abelard sent Héloïse to the convent at Argenteuil to protect her from the vengeance of Fulbert, who was enraged by their liaison. Abelard himself was the victim of a revenge attack (by whose family it is uncertain): he was taken from his bed and castrated. After that he became a monk at the Abbey of St Denis.

Thomas Aquinas: *Doctor Angelicus*

Thomas Aquinas's early life was irregular, including a period of house arrest by his mother, who did not wish him to join the

Dominican order of monks (she wanted him to be a Benedictine). He became a brilliant writer and teacher who essentially codified the canon of Christian teaching by the time he had reached his forties, in a massive work known as the *Summa Theologica* (1265–74). It is an accomplishment comparable to Maimonides' *Mishneh Torah*.

A few months before his death, Aquinas reported that Jesus Christ had spoken to him while he was celebrating Mass on 6 December 1273. Christ, he said, had asked him what he wished for as recompense for his good deeds, and Aquinas had replied, 'Only you, Lord. Only you.'

> It would seem that several angels can be at the same time in the same place. For several bodies cannot be at the same time in the same place, because they fill the place. But angels do not fill a place, because only a body fills a place, so that it be not empty, as appears from the Philosopher [Aristotle] (*Phys.* iv, text. 52, 58). Therefore several angels can be in one place.
>
> Thomas Aquinas, *Summa Theologica* (1265–74), 'Third Article: Whether Several Angels Can Be at the Same Time in the Same Place?' (trans. Fathers of English Dominican Province, 1911)

Aquinas was a master of rhetoric and used his thorough knowledge of Aristotelian logic to write what amounted to a handbook of arguments in support of Christian doctrine. These arguments were designed to assist Christians in debate with those who shared common texts – for instance, Jews who based their arguments on the Old Testament, and Christian heretics who used the New Testament. They were also designed to counter the arguments of Muslims and pagans. The *Summa Theologica* is a masterpiece of logical argument. It shows the greatest mind of the period put to the task of building a grand edifice of religious belief that includes a full account of God, angels, man and creation. While from the standpoint of the scientific observer the existence of angels is doubtful, Aquinas nevertheless used Aristotelian logic to construct a system of belief that has sustained Roman Catholicism for more than 700 years.

Aquinas contributed five major arguments that may be seen as the bedrock of Scholasticism. The first is the unmoved mover: things that move in the world must be moved by something, and in turn by something else again. The second argument is that nothing is caused by itself: I am the author of this book, my parents are the author of me, and so on. The trap of infinite regress is avoided by saying that God is the first cause of everything. The third argument is the cosmological argument: in the context of infinite time, things come into and out of existence, and there must have been a time when there was nothing, but since nothing cannot cause anything, God is the eternal cause of everything. The fourth argument says that varying degrees of attributes such as goodness are established by comparison with God, the standard of goodness. The fifth and most famous argument is the teleological argument (sometimes called the argument from design): all movement is teleological or moves towards an end, so there must be a force that directs this motion, namely God.

> The existence of the spiritual, non-corporeal beings that Sacred Scripture usually calls 'angels' is a truth of faith. The witness of Scripture is as clear as the unanimity of Tradition.
>
> *Catechism of the Catholic Church* (second edition, 1994)

Duns Scotus and Ockham's razor

While Aquinas's work could be said to be Aristotelian in character, there was another Scholastic tradition, represented by John Duns Scotus (*c.*1266–1308) and William of Ockham (*c.*1285–*c.*1349), that challenged some essential components of Thomism. Scotus was a Scottish priest who made his reputation at Cambridge and Oxford universities before going to the University of Paris, where he was regent master of theology – a duty that required the holder to lecture undergraduates on biblical scripture. Scotus was a metaphysician who developed a realist position that would influence twentieth-century thinkers such as Heidegger and C. S. Peirce. He was interested – as had been Plato and others before him – in transcendental categories, including not only *being* but ideas of the *one*, of *truth* and *good* – and the relations that might obtain among them, such as causality. What distinguishes Scotus from other Scholastic thinkers is his concern with the concept of *individuation*, the idea of the specificity of *this* thing rather than *that* thing – the *thisness* of things and persons that makes each one unique. Scotus used the term *haecceitas* to refer to his concept of *thisness*.

His preoccupation with uniqueness led Scotus to a realist position in which his focus on individual persons acknowledged their freedom, in contrast to the determinism that some inferred from God's foreknowledge of things to come. He believed that the urge of human freedom was to turn towards justice. Scotus was called *Doctor Subtilis* on account of his ability to make subtle distinctions among categories (though rather unfairly, his critics coined the term 'dunce' – from *dunsman* or follower of Duns – which later became a term of abuse, to refer to someone who is stupid, hence the dunce's cap).

The other thinker of this period famous for razor-fine distinctions is the English Franciscan friar William of Ockham. Unlike Scotus, Ockham was not a realist but a nominalist – that is, a proponent of the theory of knowledge that denies the existence of abstract concepts or universals. Ockham also rejected logical proofs of the existence of God, separating the concepts of faith and knowledge. He is most famous for the principle that bears his name, *Ockham's razor*, which generally recommends that in explaining a thing no more assumptions should be made than are absolutely necessary.

Death for heretics

Scholasticism wasn't just an exercise in logical thinking. Thomas's summation of Church views on all matters included positions regarding *just war* and the death penalty for heretics. Here, the perennial conflict between knowledge and belief reaches a defining moment. For Thomas, one must either subscribe to Christian belief or face death. The Inquisition required local authorities to establish tribunals to try cases of heresy. Those found guilty were executed by the secular authority. The belief that Thomas demands is very specifically the Church's *exact* belief. Simply declaring oneself a Christian who follows Christ's example does not meet the Thomist standard of faith.

While Thomas's logic is valid, its truth depends upon the acceptance of premises that a sceptic might reject as unproven: for instance, the existence of God. Ultimately, the truths of religion rest upon revelation, not the rigour of logical construction. For those willing to subscribe to Thomas's clearly (but narrowly) defined system of belief, Scholastic thought is breathtaking in its achievements. For those unwilling to accept the premise of a belief in God and the narrow strictures of Thomism, Thomist doctrine must be seen as the enemy of philosophical inquiry. Thomas's unwillingness to accept philosophy as an equal path to truth reveals a schism far broader than any ecclesiastical ones: that between reason and belief. It is a stand-off that continues to this day.

Inherent in Thomist thought is a disregard for the views of others who do not share the same beliefs: not only Jews and Muslims, but a large number of people born into Christian society who only partially accept – or wholly reject – Church doctrine.

By contrast, Jewish law, as codified by Maimonides, places reason before belief in the matter of the death penalty. He wrote in the *Book of Commandments*: 'It is better and more satisfactory to acquit a thousand guilty persons than to put a single innocent one to death.' Maimonides certainly did not advocate putting someone to death because they disagreed with his religious views (indeed, one of the appealing features of Judaism is its tradition of Torah study and disputation, which allows for disagreement as an essential part of religious inquiry). Even in a civil context, Maimonides objected to the death penalty because absolute certainty of guilt was an unattainable burden of proof, and he feared – just as opponents of the death penalty do today – that prosecutorial caprice and other extra-legal factors could come into play. Unlike Maimonides, the Church authorities were certain that heresy could reliably be identified and its perpetrators dealt with 'justly'.

Albigensians and Hussites: the enemies within

On occasion the Church's method of dealing with heresy went beyond repression and erupted into war. By the late twelfth century, the Cathar heresy was becoming a mass movement in southwestern France. (The Cathars were often referred to as Albigensians, because many of them lived in or near the city of Albi in Languedoc.) Catharism contained echoes of Manichaeism, its adherents holding that there were two gods: an evil one who ruled the physical world, and a good one who was incorporeal and represented spiritual perfection. At the heart of the movement a religious elite of *parfaits* ('perfects') lived lives of extreme asceticism, avoiding sexual contact and the eating of meat. Cathars renounced marriage, did not own private property and believed in reincarnation in a manner that has led some to compare them to Buddhists. In their view, they were faithfully following the example of Jesus Christ; in the view of the papacy, they represented a serious threat to the authority of the Church.

When peaceful attempts at conversion by Dominican monks failed to persuade the Cathars to renounce their heretical beliefs and rejoin the Church, Pope Innocent III (1160/1–1216) called for a Crusade against them, which would be prosecuted with enthusiastic brutality by mainly French armies. Their motives were far from pious: Innocent had decreed that the Cathars' substantial landholdings in the south of France would become the property of any French nobleman willing to heed the call to arms.

It took the Church twenty years to root out Catharism, a heresy mentioned here largely because it gave rise to the Inquisition. The Inquisition was an ecclesiastical tribunal by means of which the Church rooted out and punished heresy. Punishments ranged from imprisonment and torture to the death penalty. The methods of execution could be extremely cruel – such as burning at the stake – so as to warn would-be heretics that the Church would not tolerate dissension in religious thought or practice. The Inquisition lasted for more than 600 years and is divided into four main phases. The *Medieval Inquisition* began just after the end of the Albigensian Crusade in 1231 and extended into the sixteenth century. The *Spanish Inquisition*, begun in 1478, extended all the way into the nineteenth century, ending in 1834; the *Portuguese Inquisition*, too, lasted from 1536 to 1821; and the Roman Inquisition began in 1542 and ended around 1860. The Spanish and Portuguese Inquisitions were largely concerned with rooting out Judaism and Islam. The Roman Inquisition challenged the ideas of the Protestant Reformation, and of Renaissance humanism, which it viewed – correctly, as it turns out – as dangerous to the survival of the Church.

The Albigensian Crusade was an attack by the forces of Catholic orthodoxy on a heretical 'enemy within'. Most of the Crusades initiated by the Church during the medieval period, however, were aimed at the extirpation or conversion of heathens: the nine Crusades despatched to Palestine between 1098 and 1271 had as their aim the reclaiming of the Christian holy places from the clutches of Islam; while the Northern Crusades of the twelfth and thirteenth centuries were undertaken by the Christian Danes, Swedes and German military orders against various pagan peoples of northeastern Europe.

Some two centuries after the suppression of the Cathars, a conflict broke out in Central Europe, the ecclesiastical and theological ramifications of which were rather more ominous for the Church than earlier events in Languedoc. The underlying causes of the Hussite Wars (1419–c.1434) – launched by papal forces against the supporters of the reforming Bohemian cleric Jan Hus (c.1369–1415) – prefigure the Protestant Reformation that would spell the end of the dominance of the Roman Church in Europe in the following century. Hus was burned at the stake for believing – like his fellow reformer, the English theologian and philosopher John Wycliffe (c.1328–84), whose teachings exerted a strong influence on him – that the Church consisted not just in the clergy, but in its communicants as well. He was against the sale of indulgences (pardon of sins in return for money) and the Crusader movement. Hus was also an early advocate of the separation of church and state powers, and held that the Pope had no right to inflict violence on persons, irrespective of their religious beliefs.

The twelfth-century Renaissance

While the Inquisition and the Crusades were inimical to free thought, the medieval period has increasingly been seen to have offered some important antecedents to the Italian Renaissance, which began at the end of the thirteenth century and transformed the intellectual, cultural and commercial face of Europe. Historians have identified three such moments of cultural renewal during the medieval period: the Carolingian Renaissance of the eighth and ninth centuries; the tenth-century Ottonian Renaissance (which flourished under the rule of the Saxon Ottonian dynasty in Central and Southern Europe); and the much wider-ranging twelfth-century Renaissance. It is this last renaissance that prepared the way for the fully fledged Italian Renaissance, and other renaissances that followed in England, France, Germany and, eventually, throughout Europe.

The most visible legacy of the twelfth-century Renaissance is the achievement of the architectural style then known as *Opus Francigenum* or the French style, which eventually became known as Gothic. Perhaps the best-known example of Gothic architecture is Notre Dame Cathedral in Paris, which includes paradigm examples of three defining characteristics of the style: flying buttresses, pointed arches and ribbed vaults. The Gothic style wasn't just reserved for cathedrals, but was used in castles and palaces throughout Europe. It was more than just a way of designing buildings. The Gothic style embodied the loftiest aspirations of man at the service of God: rooting them on a sound footing, while soaring to great heights with arches that defied space.

We learned from the ancient Greeks that ideas always travel with trade. As trade accelerated in the twelfth century, so did the spread of ideas, particularly via the Hanseatic League (a trading alliance of north German cities), and the opening of the Silk Road, the main trade route to China, by the Venetian explorer Marco Polo (*c*.1254–*c*.1324). The importance of the Silk Road did not lie solely in its connection to China. It linked Southern and Eastern Europe with the Near East and Southeast Asia as it passed through what are now Egypt, Iran, Pakistan, Vietnam and Indonesia.

Technological innovations that resulted from an understanding of scientific principles drove the wealth that could be created from the new trade alliances and distribution networks. The windmill, paper factories and the spinning wheel all contributed to this growth. Two navigation tools – the magnetic compass and the astrolabe – enabled human travel and the transportation of goods.

The Italian Renaissance

One of the key elements in the spread of new ideas during the Italian Renaissance was the development of literature written in the vernacular. By writing in the language of the people – for example, Italian – instead of Latin, authors contributed to the development of a sense of national identity and unity. While it was not until the nineteenth century that Italian city-states were joined into one national entity (1815–71), a sense of *being* Italian derived from reading such works as *The Divine Comedy* by Dante Alighieri (1265–1321), *The Decameron* by Giovanni Boccaccio (1313–75) or the vernacular sonnets of Petrarch (1304–74). These works of literature were not only written in the native tongue, they helped to define it. What Dante, Boccaccio and Petrarch were doing for Italian, Geoffrey Chaucer (*c.*1340–1400) did for English with *The Canterbury Tales* at the end of the fourteenth century. These works acknowledge the preoccupations of clerics, but were focused on life as lived by people of all stations, which was often presented in an earthy manner.

The idea of reading for entertainment rather than purely for instruction rapidly gained in appeal. One could argue that the Black Death – an outbreak of bubonic plague that swept Europe between 1347 and 1351 – had a part to play in the demand for distracting literary entertainment. For more than a millennium the good news story of Christianity had promised relief from the misery of this world through eternal life in heaven. Since Christ walked the Earth, much had changed. Instead of looking forward to death and the end the world, as early Christians had done, the new Europeans of the Renaissance embraced life for its own sake, celebrating human existence for its joys and accomplishments, not solely as a conduit to God. One effect of the Black Death was to make people value life more, contributing to a 'live for today' attitude in a world in which, as Boccaccio is supposed to have famously remarked, people 'ate lunch with their friends and dinner with their ancestors in paradise'.

The emergence of popular literature was made possible by a new industry: publishing. Until then, philosophy – or any kind of study involving reading – had been largely confined to an elite group. It was not only that the number of readers was in short supply, but also that there were few texts available. The ancient Greeks wrote on wax or clay tablets with a stylus, resulting in a single, perishable original. The Chinese invented paper and their first moveable type press dates to around 1040, a good four centuries before the German goldsmith Johannes Gutenberg (*c*.1398–1468) 'invented' it. However, his invention quickened the spread of ideas because it allowed for multiple copies of books to be created quickly and at relatively low cost. It also removed control over the creation and distribution of books from the the Church and the state, and introduced them to the free market. Boccaccio's *Decameron*, first printed in 1470 (it had previously circulated in manuscript), was an early example of what would follow.

The enduring legacy of Greece and Rome

Ideas, like diseases, are spread by great movements of people. The fall of Constantinople to the Ottoman Turks in 1453 marked the end of the Byzantine (or Eastern Roman) Empire, which had ruled for more than a thousand years. In response to Muslim rule, many Greeks fled to Italy. This contributed further to a European interest in antiquity that had far-reaching consequences. For instance, the reintroduction of Greek ideas fuelled a philhellenism that would later inspire Europeans like the English Romantic poet Lord Byron (1788–1824) to support Greek independence from the Ottomans (Byron died of sepsis while fighting for that cause). In Britain, Hellenic ideas informed the culture of the nineteenth-century public school, so helping to create the character of the English ruling class at home and in its overseas empire.

The enduring intellectual legacy of the study of Greek and Roman literary texts was humanism, a view that places the happiness and welfare of people above all else. A key figure in the spread of humanism was Marsilio Ficino (1433–99), who was the first to translate the complete works of Plato into Latin. Ficino was a truly 'Renaissance man' in that he was learned in the arts, sciences and theology. His most important work was *Theologica Platonica* (1482), a development of the idea of the Great Chain of Being, which placed man at the centre of the universe. Instead of a hierarchy with God at the top and chaos below, Ficino's system focused on the central position of man, whose goal is the ascent of the soul towards God.

Philosophy, science and invention

During the Italian Renaissance secular ideas began to compete with religious teaching on equal grounds. A new breed of thinkers would arise, informed by the philosophy of the ancient Greeks, who could now construct better theories of the nature of the universe and its creation by conducting investigations based on observation and measurement. The thirteenth-century Englishman Roger Bacon (*c*.1214–*c*.1294) was a Franciscan friar and an early advocate of scientific method, who laboured under the nickname of *Doctor Mirabilis* ('wonderful teacher'). In 1267 Bacon presented to Pope Clement IV (at the Pope's request) a manuscript of his *Opus Majus* ('great work'), which outlined his scientific method and put it in the context of theological and philosophical thought. It was not published in its entirety until 1897. Bacon's work would create a new standard for knowledge, in which hypotheses were formulated and proved or disproved by experimentation.

The great Renaissance polymath Nicholas of Cusa (1401–64) embodied the two competing strands of belief and knowledge that have marked philosophical inquiry from the beginning. Nicholas was a German cardinal who was both an original thinker in theology and a scientist whose predictions in astronomy predated discoveries that would later be confirmed by observation. He challenged the prevailing Aristotelian model of the cosmos and anticipated Johannes Kepler's (1571–1630) theory that the planets orbit the sun elliptically, and not in a circle. Nicholas worked out a mathematical proposition that since no perfect circle exists in the universe, the planets must therefore have elliptical orbits. He developed the theological concept of *learned ignorance*, which outlined his notion of a supra-rational understanding that goes beyond the rational powers of the human mind.

Leonardo da Vinci (1452–1519) is the Renaissance figure par excellence. Perhaps best known as an artist (painter and sculptor),

Leonardo also added science and mathematics to his arsenal of tools for understanding. It was the marriage of art and science in Leonardo's work that defined this new period in Western thought. Thinkers, increasingly freed from the constraints of Church dogma, were able to reconceptualize problems that had hitherto been misrepresented by the requirement that they conform to the demands of belief.

Leonardo's imagination as an artist and his observational discipline as a scientist gave him the ability to invent. And invent he did – his work includes the earliest designs for the helicopter and the tank. Inventions not only made life easier, they also generated large profits. And invention led to production, which in turn led to the creation of markets and a network of transportation to serve those markets. It led to the amassing of capital and the creation of secular power separate from that of the Church and nobility. Invention would give rise to the middle class, which would become a new source of ideas, as well as a receptive market for them. It would also transform thought. From now on, thinkers would not simply be philosophers: they would also be scientists who made theory and inventors who made technology. They would eventually be joined by social scientists: economists, psychologists and sociologists.

Invention also changed the nature of warfare, which was the inevitable result of a new European imperialism. Invention would speed up transportation, and lead to the development of weapons that increased the distance between killer and killed. For example, the earliest warfare was hand-to-hand, in which one bludgeoned or cut one's opponent to death; killing by projecting missiles at one's enemy from a safe position was restricted to various permutations of the slingshot. The introduction of gunpowder in Western Europe in the thirteenth century meant that guns and canon increased the distance from which one could kill. From the late fifteenth century onwards, the pitting of Spanish conquistadors armed with guns against the traditionally armed indigenous peoples of the New World would set in motion an expansion of markets and ideas that now drives our global economy.

1492

The year 1492 was an *annus mirabilis* or an *annus horribilis*, depending upon your point of view. It was a 'year of wonders' for the ragtag band of adventurers under the command of Christopher Columbus (*c.*1451–1506), who sailed under the Spanish flag and was funded by Queen Isabella I of Castile. Before he set off for the New World, Columbus witnessed an event of real consequence for world history: the surrender of Muhammad XII of Granada (*c.*1460–*c.*1533), popularly known as Boabdil, the twenty-second (and last) ruler of the emirate of Granada. Boabdil's surrender (the culmination of the Reconquista), which ended 800 years of Muslim rule in southern Spain, was a blow to Islamic ambitions in Europe. (Though from the seizure of Constantinople in 1453 until 1683, the Ottoman Turks remained an expansionist power in southeastern Europe.)

Columbus's journey to the New World would mean untold wealth for the conquistadors and a new market for Christian missionaries. Unfortunately, it meant death for the indigenous peoples of the Americas through military action and the new diseases the conquerors brought with them (chiefly smallpox). In the wake of Columbus, a steady stream of adventurers and explorers continued the process of Western European expropriation of the Americas, including the Spaniards Hernán Cortés (1485–1547) and Francisco Pizarro (c.1471–1541) in Mexico and Peru respectively, and the Frenchman Samuel de Champlain (c.1567–1635) in North America.

By contrast, 1492 was a horrible year for the Jews and Muslims of Spain. One of the first acts of the Spanish monarchs Ferdinand and Isabella was the Alhambra decree, which gave Spanish Jews the option of converting to Roman Catholicism or being expelled; 150,000 left Spain in July 1492. Many Muslims, given the same 'choice', elected to remain in Spain as notional Catholics, but retaining Arabic language, dress and customs (they were known as Moriscos).

Rather better news for Jews in 1492 was the publication in Lisbon, in Portugal, of an edition of the Torah or the Pentateuch (the Five Books of Moses). Also, in an act of generosity guided by self-interest, the Ottoman sultan Bayezid II (1447–1512) rescued the expelled Jews and Muslims of Spain by sending his navy to bring them to safety, with most of the Jews settling in Greece and Turkey. He ordered that Jews be welcomed throughout his empire, and extended to them the rights of Ottoman citizenship. The self-interest of Bayezid's action was made plain when he praised the learning and skills of the Spanish Jews, while questioning the wisdom of the Spanish rulers in making their kingdom poorer and enriching his own. (The United States would similarly benefit from Jewish immigration resulting from the anti-Semitic actions of the German government between 1933 and 1945.)

Martin Luther and the Protestant Reformation

The Protestant Reformation came about because of disgust at abuses within the Church, which was increasingly regarded as corrupt and worldly. Criticisms first came from the followers of John Wycliffe in England in the late fourteenth century (known as Lollards), then from the Hussites of Bohemia in the early fifteenth, but the start of the Reformation is usually dated to 1517, when the Augustinian monk Martin Luther (1483–1546) published his opposition to indulgences and other clerical abuses. Some priests who were similarly concerned about the Church's direction of travel – men like Erasmus (1466–1536), the Dutch humanist scholar and author of *In Praise of Folly* (1509), a satirical examination of Catholic doctrine and corrupt ecclesiastical practices – would never make common cause with the Reformers, and endeavoured to reform the Church from within. Luther, however, embarked on a rather more radical path.

His criticisms of the Church were not focused simply on its sale of indulgences, but extended to its teachings as a whole. Luther believed that Christ's teaching was better understood through individual study of the Bible, and not through the catechism of Church belief, an elaborate edifice that had been created by medieval scholars. Essentially, Luther believed that salvation came about through a direct relationship with God.

> A Christian man is the most free lord of all, and subject to none; a Christian man is the most dutiful servant of all, and is subject to everyone.
>
> Martin Luther, *Concerning Christian Liberty* (1520)
> (trans. R. S. Grignon, 1885)

This marked one of the major turning-points in Western thought and history, much as Augustine's *Confessions* had done a thousand years before. Luther emphasized, as did Augustine in his first-person writing, the growing power of the individual. Luther's translation of the Bible into German (New Testament, 1522; Old Testament, 1534) made the word of God available to people in their own language (and helped nudge the German language into a 'standard form'). Luther's translation also influenced other vernacular Bible translations, including William Tyndale's (*c.* 1492–1536) English Bible, which began to be published in parts from 1525 (copies were printed in Germany and the Netherlands, then smuggled into England), as well as the King James version (1611), both of which advanced the growth of the English language. These translations introduced the Bible into popular culture for the first time. As a result it became widely read as literature, as much as for its religious content, thereby creating the common ground of what we now call the Judaeo-Christian tradition in the West. Western thought owes an enormous debt to Tyndale. For his pains, the Church had him strangled at the stake, and his corpse was burned.

I defy the Pope, and all his laws; and if God spares my life, ere many years, I will cause the boy that driveth the plow to know more of the Scriptures than thou dost!

William Tyndale, in Foxe's *Book of Martyrs* (1563)

The word of God had been made available to the people in their own language – that was the essential difference between the Protestants and the Church of Rome. Much like the Talmudic tradition in Judaism, the Protestant movement encouraged a critical reading of scripture. If Talmudic study may be seen as the beginning of hermeneutics, the translation of the Bible into the vernacular is a further stage in its development. Vernacular translations of the Bible not only led to an increase in the study of theology as a crucial branch of knowledge, but to more widespread literacy and the growth of knowledge in general.

The Lutheran Church spread rapidly in Germany and Northern Europe, and influenced the emerging Anglican Church in England. Reform was also carried out in Switzerland by Ulrich Zwingli (1484–1531) and Jean Calvin (1509–64), who established the Calvinist Church. The challenge of Protestantism led the Catholic Church to conduct its own Reformation (often referred to as the Counter-Reformation), establishing the Council of Trent (1545–63) to reform the Church from within. The religious and political changes that followed the onset of the Reformation unleashed a series of wars that would destabilize Western Europe for more than a hundred years, from the mid-1520s to the mid-seventeenth century.

The liberation of the individual

The liberation of the individual that resulted from a combination of the Renaissance, the Reformation, and the scientific revolution was the precondition for the great economic growth of the seventeenth century, as well as political changes that would lead, ultimately, to republicanism: the rule of men by men who did not regard themselves as divinely appointed. All of these great changes were facilitated by the free flow of ideas that came from the printing press: books in great numbers in all the vernacular languages of Europe – Italian, French, German, Spanish, Portuguese and English.

These books included works of theology, science, mathematics and philosophy; epic romances by the Italian poets Ludovico Ariosto (1474 –1533) and Torquato Tasso (1544–95); prose satires by the rumbustious Frenchman François Rabelais (c.1494–c.1553); Portugal's national epic, *The Lusiads* (1572), by Luís de Camões (1524–80); dramas and sonnets by England's national poet William Shakespeare (1564–1616); and the chivalric satire *Don Quixote* (1605 and 1615) by the Spaniard Miguel de Cervantes (1547–1616). Each of these writers helped to mould their respective national identities.

A Renaissance writer who seems to look forward to the next great intellectual movement, the Enlightenment, is the Frenchman Michel de Montaigne (1533–92), best known for his *Essais* (1580). The title means 'attempts', and marks the birth of a new literary form in which ideas could be given concise expression and wide dissemination due to their brevity (and the cheapness of producing copies). Montaigne's work is the culmination of important Renaissance and Reformation advances. It is a new and popular literary form, written in the vernacular and published widely. The subjects of Montaigne's 107 essays are remarkably diverse and include rethinking of classical ideas along with the promulgation of new ones. His topics include idleness, procrastination, liars, sadness, constancy, fear, moderation, Cato the Younger, and thumbs. Montaigne addresses cannibalism, the affection of fathers for their children, and the disadvantages of high rank. Though a sceptic and a pessimist, Montaigne is highly entertaining. He is best remembered for his phrase *Que sais-je?* ('What do I know?'). Montaigne's focus on the first person advanced the tradition that started with Augustine's *Confessions*, and influenced Descartes and his *cogito*: *I think, therefore I am.*

Not only does the wind of chance events shake me about as it lists, but I also shake and disturb myself by the instability of my stance: anyone who turns his prime attention on to himself will hardly ever find himself in the same state twice.

Michel de Montaigne, *Essais* (1580)

(trans. M. A. Screech, 1987)

Index Librorum Prohibitorum

As more ideas reached more people, the Catholic Church began to lose its power over them. In 1559 Pope Paul IV had ordered the creation of the *Index Librorum Prohibitorum*, a list of books that Catholics were forbidden to read; Montaigne's *Essais* would be among them. The Church's method of control now moved from the body to the mind. It replaced the murder of the Crusades and torture of the Inquisition with a form of mind control that lasted until 1966. A brief summary of the authors outlawed by the Church shows that it forbade Catholics to read a significant number of the core texts of Western thought, analytical philosophy excluded: Galileo Galilei (1564–1642), Francis Bacon (1561–1626), Johannes Kepler, René Descartes (1596–1650), Blaise Pascal (1623–62), John Locke (1632–1704), Voltaire (1694–1778), Jean-Jacques Rousseau (1712–78), Denis Diderot (1713–84), David Hume (1711–76), Immanuel Kant (1724–1804), Henri Bergson (1859–1941), Jean-Paul Sartre (1905–80), Simone de Beauvoir (1908–86). It can be seen that the Church was particularly punishing towards the French. The *Index*, oddly, omitted Friedrich Nietzsche (1844–1900), the great critic of Christian morals. Perhaps easier to understand is its omission of *Mein Kampf* by Adolf Hitler (1889–1945), given the Church's long history of anti-Semitism; but the omission of the works of Karl Marx

(1818–83), the most influential anti-Christian in modern times, is puzzling.

As can readily be seen, the fact that every name listed above was widely read by contemporaries – and is still read today – shows that the Church's efforts to stifle independent thought were a failure. The Protestant Reformation and the various European renaissances opened the floodgates. Free thinking would lead to a demand for liberation from despots, be they kings or clerics. From now on, reason would play a greater role in governance of every stripe.

PART THREE

The Scientific Revolution

16th century to 18th century

In the year of his death Nicolaus Copernicus (1473–1543), a German born in what is now Poland, published *On the Revolutions of the Heavenly Spheres*, which demonstrated that the earth, like the other planets, revolved around the sun, and not vice versa. It was a truly revolutionary work, because it put paid once and for all to Ptolemy's (*c.*AD 90–*c.*168) geocentric model, which placed the earth at the centre of the universe. The other revolutionary book of 1543 was Andreas Vesalius's (1514–64) *On the Fabric of the Human Body*, the first modern study of human anatomy, which would eventually overturn the humoural pathology handed down from Aristotle to Galen. Both publications were revolutionary because they overturned existing doctrine, and both challenged the power of the Church, which strictly controlled the universities in which astronomy and medicine were taught. But leaving aside the conflicts with the Church – all science would be ultimately in conflict with the Church – Copernicus gave us a new understanding of that which is *outside* us, in space, while Vesalius did the same for what happens *inside* us. These two discoveries of the *without* and the *within* mark the beginning of the Scientific Revolution.

Nicolaus Copernicus was a Renaissance polymath. In addition to being a mathematician and astronomer, he was a physician, diplomat, military leader, economist and more. He was an amateur astronomer, yet his work on the heliocentric solar system was his most enduring legacy. Vesalius, on the other hand, was a physician; and while physicians might also be philosophers and artists, they were typically scientists first and foremost. Until well into the modern period, physicians were the leading group of professional scientists, because there were more sick people willing to pay for their treatment than kings willing to pay a ransom to employ a house astronomer.

> . . . as far as hypotheses go, let no one expect anything in the way of certainty from astronomy, since astronomy can offer us nothing certain, lest, if anyone take as true that which has been constructed for another use, he go away from this discipline a bigger fool than when he came to it.
>
> Nicolaus Copernicus, *On the Revolutions of the Heavenly Spheres* (1543) (trans. Charles Glen Wallis, 1939)

Tools for doing science

The discoveries of Copernicus and Vesalius were the products of reason, not revelation or the mystical or numerological speculation of Nicholas of Cusa. They used philosophical reflection to create testable hypotheses that led to further research and experimentation. The greatest of the naked-eye astronomers – those who worked before the introduction of the telescope in 1608 – was the Danish nobleman Tycho Brahe (1546–1601). In 1573 he published *De Nova Stella* (*On the New Star*), his account of sighting and making calculations about a supernova which is known to present-day astronomers as SN 1572 (or, more poetically, Tycho's Supernova). Until now, Aristotle and Ptolemy had taught that the stars had been created by God and constituted a fixed, unchanging universe. Based on measurements taken with the naked eye, Brahe's calculations replaced that belief with scientific fact. His assistant, the German Johannes Kepler, was one of the first astronomers to use the telescope (though he benefited greatly from Brahe's naked-eye observations). Kepler discovered the mathematical laws that govern planetary motion (Kepler's Laws), which he outlined in *Epitome of Copernican Astronomy* (1617–21).

Increasingly, scientific knowledge based on fact had Christian belief and even the institution of the Church itself on the run.

The very existence of the telescope, a tool for exploring the *extraterrestrial*, challenged the Church's claim to the territory of heaven, home to God and the angels, hidden to man until his death and subsequent rebirth through Jesus Christ.

> Now we, thanks to the telescope, have brought the heavens thirty or forty times closer to us than they were to Aristotle, so that we can discern many things in them that he could not see; among other things these sunspots, which were absolutely invisible to him. Therefore we can treat of the heavens and the sun more confidently than Aristotle could.
>
> Galileo Galilei, *Dialogue Concerning the Two Chief World Systems* (1632) (trans. Stillman Drake, 1953)

The telescope, like its cousin the microscope, was invented by Dutch spectacle makers. Several of them had a hand in its invention: Hans Lippershey (1570–1619), Zacharias Janssen (*c*.1580–*c*.1638) and Jacob Metius (*c*.1571–1630). The first telescope appeared in 1608 and was modified by Galileo Galilei (1564–1642), who used it to confirm by observation Copernicus's heliocentric model of the solar system. Galileo's contributions were many, and the theoretical physicist Stephen Hawking (*b*.1942) has said that modern science begins with Galileo. But for our purposes he is chiefly remembered for his support of the heliocentric view of the universe. Most scientists (or natural philosophers) followed the Church's view that the earth, not the sun, was the centre of the universe. Galileo was denounced to the Roman Inquisition in 1615. On this occasion he was not found guilty in a plea bargain that gave him his freedom if he renounced his views. But Galileo continued his researches and in 1632 published his best-known work, the *Dialogue Concerning the Two Chief World Systems*, in which he offered convincing arguments for heliocentrism. He was retried by the Inquisition and sentenced to house arrest for the rest of his life. The *Dialogue* was placed on the Church's *Index* of proscribed books, where it remained until 1835. It is perhaps in the case of Galileo more than any other thinker that we see the Church using its considerable power to force belief in doctrinaire orthodoxy over the rationally argued proofs of science. It is here that a line is drawn in the sand: the tug of war between progress and regression, between belief and knowledge, continues to this day.

While the telescope was a tool for looking past what our naked eye could see in the larger world, the microscope was a tool for looking within, to search for that which is invisible due to its smallness. The invention of the microscope is usually credited to the Dutch spectacle-maker Zacharias Janssen in 1590; but since he would have been ten years old at the time, it seems likely that his father, Hans, had a hand in it. As with all tools, the microscope is only as good as those who use it, and the first to exploit its full potential was Antonie van Leeuwenhoek (1632–1723), who used it to 'discover' red blood cells in 1674. Or perhaps I should say 'rediscover', because they had already been described by his fellow Dutchman Jan Swammerdam (1637–80) in his work on frog's blood in 1658, although van Leeuwenhoek was unaware of this. Simultaneous (or near simultaneous) discovery is common throughout the history of science. For example, a version of the theory of evolution was formulated by Alfred Russel Wallace (1823–1913) simultaneously with and independently of Charles Darwin; penicillin was discovered by the French physician Ernest Duchesne (1874–1912) in 1896 (while he was still a medical student), but its rediscovery in 1928 by the more famous British bacteriologist Alexander Fleming (1881–1955) got more notice. Van Leeuwenhoek's 'discovery' of blood corpuscles contributed to a movement away from the old Aristotelian picture of the world as being composed of the four elements of air, water, fire and earth, towards a new understanding of the world as composed of atoms and corpuscles. Van Leeuwenhoek was the first microbiologist, leading the exploration into the interior world of increasingly smaller units of matter. He was the first to observe sperm cells, the origin of us all.

The new relationship of philosophy and science

A recurring figure in the history of science is the gentleman practitioner or enlightened amateur, epitomized by the Englishman Francis Bacon (1561–1626); other notable examples include Copernicus and the English physicist Isaac Newton (1643–1727), who was also a Member of Parliament, warden of the Royal Mint, Chancellor of the Exchequer, Attorney General and Lord Chancellor of England.

Bacon's great work is *Novum Organum* (1620), a 'new instrument' for doing science. He argued that scientific investigation must be rooted in what we perceive with our senses, as opposed to accepting any a priori assumptions (independent of experience). His method was based on a form of logic known as eliminative induction. It is a method by which a number of competing hypotheses to explain a phenomenon are entertained, the number then being reduced by the discovery of new evidence that eliminates them.

> They who have presumed to dogmatize on Nature, as on some well-investigated subject, either from self-conceit or arrogance, and in the professorial style, have inflicted the greatest injury on Philosophy and Learning.
>
> Francis Bacon, *Novum Organum* (1620)
>
> (trans. Joseph Devey, 1901)

Democritus and Aristotle were philosophers who did science without fancy tools. Kepler and Galileo used the new tools of science to help solve questions asked by philosophers. In our era, Stephen Hawking has proclaimed that philosophy is dead, because science has answered all of its questions. He is wrong: the relationship between science and philosophy is too vital, and too mutually beneficial, for it to be driven asunder by one claiming primacy over the other. We still need philosophy to help us study the question 'what is mind?'. Although neurophysics can create electrochemical maps of the brain, these do not equate to the mind. One job of philosophers today is to keep the cat alive, while scientists try to isolate the source of its purr.

> How can we understand the world in which we find ourselves? . . . Did the universe have a creator? Traditionally these are questions for philosophy, but philosophy is dead.
>
> Stephen Hawking and Leonard Mlodinow,
> *The Grand Design: New Answers to the*
> *Ultimate Questions of Life* (2010)

New scientific breakthroughs give rise to new areas of philosophy. Bioethics, for instance, is a natural philosophical response to the science of genetics and the technologies involved in such practices as gene copyrighting. Philosophy ignores science at its peril; and science, without philosophy, would lose its way, failing to ask essential questions – especially ethical ones – about the contexts in which it is practised. Philosophy provides the questions science tries to answer; and it provides the tools with which those answers are judged.

Descartes and the beginnings of the Enlightenment

The period in eighteenth-century Western thought known as the Enlightenment would bring rationality to the fore in combating Church intolerance and the despotism of kings. Seventeenth-century scientists were at the vanguard of the Enlightenment, and the most important of them was the Frenchman René Descartes (1596–1650), who showed just how closely related are the enterprises of philosophy and science.

Descartes was extremely critical of Scholasticism, which he dismissed because nothing was ever placed in *doubt*; it was an elaborate game in which Aristotelian logic was put to the service of 'proving' the nature of God and angels. Descartes was eager to explain the world mathematically and scientifically, and the ambitious nature of this enterprise can be measured by the title of his book *Le Monde* (*The World*). Written between 1629 and 1633, *The World* is an attempt at a more or less complete physics, with chapters on particles and the void, laws of motion, and a theory of light. Descartes' new ideas challenged the established Aristotelian account of matter by offering 'simple' mechanical explanations of physical phenomena. He rejected the prevailing notion of a relationship between sensory experience and objects in the world; all was simply mechanics. By showing how a world that was subject to physical laws could be described mathematically, independent of our often unreliable sensory organs, Descartes brought science much closer to the (probably unattainable) grail of objective truth. Things that could be described mathematically could be demonstrated to others, anywhere, in any language, at any time.

This scientific – or reductive – way of thinking gave rise to the modern philosophical method of radical doubt. Descartes' method, outlined in the *Discourse on Method* (1637) and discussed later in the *Meditations* (1641), was systematically to doubt everything one claimed to believe or know until one struck a bedrock of certainty. For Descartes, that certainty was the act of thinking: '*Je pense, donc je suis*' ('I think, therefore I am'). This apparently simple phrase has become known as the *cogito ergo sum* or the *cogito*. Descartes' critics might challenge his method as overly reductive, but they cannot deny that at the same time it introduced subjectivity into the mainstream of Western philosophy.

Descartes divided the world sharply into thought (ideas) and matter (extension or the occupation of space). One implication of this was a dualist position – Cartesian dualism – in which he viewed mind and body as separate, the mind being considered a sort of immaterial thing or object. For the analytic philosopher Bertrand Russell, Descartes' *cogito* was a disaster for philosophy. In *A History of Western Philosophy* (1945) Russell called it 'the first stage in a development, through Berkeley and Kant, to Fichte, for whom everything is only an emanation of the ego. This was insanity, and, from this extreme, philosophy has been attempting, ever since, to escape into the world of everyday common sense.'

> . . . it is not enough to have a good mind; the main thing is to apply it well. The greatest souls are capable of the greatest vices as well as the greatest virtues. And those who proceed only very slowly can make much greater progress, provided they always follow the right path, than do those who hurry and stray from it.
>
> René Descartes, *Discourse on Method* (1637)
> (trans. Donald A. Cress, 1980)

Spinoza, Leibniz and the uses of mathematics

Two other names must be linked with Descartes' in the development of Enlightenment philosophy: the Dutchman Baruch de

Spinoza (1632–77) and the German Gottfried Leibniz (1646–1716). Each contributed to the movement towards rationalism and the use of mathematics to make philosophical arguments. There is a pleasing symmetry in their work, because Leibniz, the mathematician, reconciled God with reason, while Spinoza, trained as a Talmudic scholar, found geometric explanations for his rules of ethics. Spinoza was excommunicated from the Jewish community of Amsterdam with the strongest possible curse, the terms of which included that 'no one may communicate with him verbally or in writing, nor show him any favour, nor stay under the same roof with him, nor be within four cubits of him, nor read anything composed or written by him'.

For as we are affected with a greater joy, we pass to a greater perfection, and consequently participate more in the divine nature. Nor can joy which is governed by the true principle of our advantage ever be evil. On the other hand, he who is led by fear, and does the good only to avoid evil, is not governed by reason.

Baruch de Spinoza, *Ethics* (1677)
(trans. Edwin Curley, 1994)

Spinoza made his living as a lens grinder in Amsterdam, refusing the offer of a post at the University of Heidelberg in order to maintain his independence. In 1663 he published *Principles of Cartesian Philosophy*, followed by works on politics and ethics. Spinoza dismissed Descartes' dualism, imagining God and Nature to be one fundamental unity. Like Descartes, however, he believed truth to be accessible through a deductive investigation using mathematics and geometry.

The American pragmatist John Dewey (1859–1952) said in a 1902 essay that Leibniz's philosophy marked 'the dawning consciousness of the modern world'. Like his English contemporary Isaac Newton, Leibniz was both a polymath and an amateur. Trained in the law, he occupied several roles in the court of Hanover, acting as counsellor, diplomat, historian and librarian. Newton, for his part, was the Lucasian Professor of Mathematics at Cambridge (a post that would be held in the late twentieth and early twenty-first centuries by Stephen Hawking) and later a treasury official. Both men conducted researches in fields outside their professional training: Leibniz in geology and physics; Newton in astronomy and biblical hermeneutics. Each could be said to have been the greatest thinker of the period in his respective country.

Underlying Leibniz's thought is a deeply held Christian faith, which impelled him to create an ingenious set of proofs to arrive at the position that the world we live in, which God created, is 'the best of all possible worlds', despite its apparent imperfections.

While that conclusion might be questionable, Leibniz's achieve-ments in mathematics are not. One of his most enduring accom-plishments – measured by its effect on twentieth-century thinkers like Russell and Frege – was his idea for a universal language of ideographic symbols that could express a very limited number of concepts upon which knowledge could be built. This is a key idea of the logicism that led to the development of the analytic tradi-tion in the twentieth century. The other was the invention of the infinitesimal calculus or, simply, calculus. Calculus is the study of change. It is a tool for making mathematical models of problems in the physical sciences, which made it useful in Newton's day when he was charting the movements of the planets. In the twenty-first century the calculus is employed to model problems in areas as diverse as medicine, demography and the behaviour of ageing nuclear weapons.

Leibniz and Newton both claimed to have invented the calculus, and the evidence suggests that they are both correct – that is, they discovered it independently. Newton said he was working with the calculus in 1666, but did not bother to publish his work at the time. Leibniz began his work with the calculus in 1674 and published his results in *Novus Methodus* (1684). Their argument high-lights the importance of timely publication of results in science and philosophy; time and again in the history of philosophy, this problem of precedence will occur.

> ... there will be no good action that is unrewarded, no bad action that goes unpunished.
>
> Gottfried Leibniz, *On the Ultimate Order of Things* (1697)
>
> (trans. Daniel Garber and Roger Ariew, 1991)

An apple falls from a tree . . .

The apple occupies two glorious moments in the history of epistemology. First, in Genesis, Eve tempts Adam to eat an apple, the forbidden fruit of the Tree of Knowledge. Adam ate it, thereby disobeying God. As a result, Adam and Eve were expelled from paradise and obliged to walk the Earth, knowing disease, disaster and death (the fruits of knowledge as advertised in the Old Testament). The other apple moment came when Isaac Newton observed one fall from a tree and asked himself the following question: if the apple on the tree was at rest, then it gradually accelerated while falling, what causes that acceleration? Newton's answer was *gravity*, the single most important idea in the history of physics. Gravity is the force that draws objects towards a mass. A mass has gravity (like our planet, whose gravity keeps our feet on the ground); the greater the mass, the greater the pull of gravity. Gravity is the unseen force which is at work when things move. The first mover is no longer the Absolute or God, it is gravity; and gravity is governed by laws that can be expressed mathematically. Newton's discovery of gravity is the first big dent in the Creation myth.

> . . . gravity, by which bodies tend to the centre of the earth; magnetism, by which iron tends to the loadstone; and that force, whatever it is, by which the planets are perpetually drawn aside from the rectilinear motions, which otherwise they would pursue, and made to revolve in curvilinear orbits.
>
> Isaac Newton, *Principia* (1687)
>
> (trans. Andrew Motte, 1995)

Newton was a strange fellow for, despite the adjective 'Newtonian' having been coined to describe the predictable, mechanical universe he outlined, he devoted much study to alchemy and theology. He believed that God had selected him as one of a few given the gift of accurate biblical exegesis. He also believed – based on evidence that would not pass muster as scientific – that the world would end in 2060.

Alchemy aside, Newton took up the methodology of Francis Bacon and, by proposing fundamental theories about how the world worked, rewrote the book on physics. Despite Einstein's twentieth-century discovery of the theory of relativity, the basic laws of physics that Newton identified are as important today as they were then, because they apply to nearly every situation we are likely to encounter (unless, that is, we are explorers of the mysterious world of subatomic particles, or supersonic seekers after information about the precise nature of the explosion that created our universe, and probably an infinite number of others ones, too).

Pascal's wager

The Enlightenment did not develop in a smooth and direct progression. Descartes' fellow countryman Blaise Pascal (1623–62) was a polymath who, if he were known only for his contributions to mathematics, would be regarded as one of the greatest. He was also an inventor who built the first mechanical calculator, a machine called the Pascaline. If that wasn't enough, he was also a theologian, which may seem curious for an Enlightenment thinker. But Pascal was an unusual theologian, and he developed a novel arithmetical approach to religious belief. After witnessing what he believed was a miracle in which his niece was cured of a condition in which pus exuded from her nose and eyes, he composed his most famous work, *Pensées* (1670). In it he expressed the view of a scientist and mathematician that Christian belief was consistent with reason. His main thesis is known as Pascal's wager. In an early exposition of what we now call *game theory*, Pascal argued that it makes more sense to believe in God than not to. The situation may be outlined as follows. If one bets on the existence of God, and it turns out He *does* exist, then one is a winner (of the ultimate prize of salvation and eternal life in Christ). If God turns out not to exist, what has been lost? Nothing. On the other hand, if one wagers that God does *not* exist, and He turns out to exist, then the consequence is damnation. So, a reasonable person, using probability and logic as his guide, chooses to believe in God.

Reason works slowly, looking so often at so many principles, which must always be present, that it is constantly nodding or straying because all its principles are not present. Feeling does not work like that, but works instantly, and is always ready. We must then put our faith in feeling, or it will always be vacillating.

Pascal, *Pensées* (1670) (trans. W. F. Trotter, 1966)

Reason and politics

The French did not have a monopoly on Enlightenment polymaths. The Englishman Thomas Hobbes (1588–1679) was an historian, geometer and scientist, in addition to being a first-rate philosopher whose principal achievements consist in elaborating a comprehensive materialist worldview, and being the father of social contract theory.

For Hobbes all knowledge was empirical – that is, it derived from what could be directly experienced by the senses – and could be reduced to the two lowest common denominators of matter and motion. As a consequence bodies and their movements are the sole subject matter of philosophy. For Hobbes, minds (or what he referred to as 'nervous systems') are bodies, too; even God is a material substance. He reduced philosophy to four areas: geometry, physics, ethics and politics. In keeping with the matter-motion rule, geometry describes the spatial movements of bodies; physics the effects of moving bodies upon one another; ethics the movement of nervous systems; and politics the effect of nervous systems upon one another.

Approaching the affairs of men with the same philosophical rigour, Hobbes created the subject we now call political science. In spite of his absolutist position, Hobbes formulated some of the basic principles of liberal philosophy. *Leviathan* (1651) is the first systematic attempt to outline a social contract between ruler and ruled, a subject further explored by Jean-Jacques Rousseau in *The Social Contract* (1762). Hobbes's materialist view led him to conclude that without proper political organization and state security to protect against enemies from without, and to regulate the internal, every-man-for-himself chaos that arises in the absence of a social contract, men would revert to a natural state in which life is 'nasty, brutish and short'.

In such condition, there is no place for industry; because the fruit thereof is uncertain: and consequently no culture of the earth; no navigation, nor use of the commodities that may be imported by sea; no commodious building; no instruments of moving, and removing, such things as require much force; no knowledge of the face of the earth; no account of time; no arts; no letters; no society; and which is worst of all, continual fear, and danger of violent death; and the life of man, solitary, poor, nasty, brutish, and short.

Thomas Hobbes, *Leviathan* (1651)

Hobbes retains an unusual relevance for contemporary thinking on the social contract issue, with key commentaries coming from John Rawls (1921–2002) in his *Theory of Justice* (1971) and Philip Pettit (*b.* 1945) in *Republicanism* (1997). In the early twenty-first century the social contract is undergoing close scrutiny as Western democracies face the combined challenges of longer life spans, unemployment and the rising cost of health care, welfare and social security programmes.

The Enlightenment: humanism at work

After Descartes, it became widespread practice in the eighteenth century to use reason to identify and solve problems, whether scientific, philosophical, social or political. The Renaissance gave us humanism, and one definition of the Enlightenment might be *humanism at work*. The Enlightenment undermined the tyranny of popes and kings, and Western Europeans began to create a new kind of society based on reason rather than revelation. Enlightenment ideas would fuel the ultimate New World experiment in governance, the United States of America.

The Enlightenment cannot be categorized in a neat, cut-and-dried way, however, because it was more a general tendency than a movement with a strict agenda; and because it rejected the shackles of religious orthodoxy, it was anti-dogmatic. The task of describing the Enlightenment is further complicated by the fact that it took different forms in different places. The centre of Enlightenment thinking was France, and there its consequences were most dramatic, culminating in the French Revolution (1789), which abolished the monarchy, dissolved the monasteries and drove a lasting wedge between church and state. But the Enlightenment took a different form in Britain, which retained its monarchy. The Scottish Enlightenment gave us David Hume (1711–76), the greatest philosopher to write in English; and the social philosopher Adam Smith (1723–90), whose *Wealth of Nations* (1776) to this day remains a standard text in classical economics. In Russia, the rule of Catherine the Great (1729–96) was perhaps the best example of the enlightened absolutism or benevolent despotism that marked the age of Enlightenment.

John Locke and empiricism

The English philosopher John Locke (1632–1704) perfected the doctrine of empiricism, which holds that all knowledge is derived from experience. That is to say, there is no such thing as an a priori proposition – something that can be known to be true or false independent of experience. (With one exception: Locke allowed that the immutable truths of geometry were given a priori.) For Locke, the human mind at birth is like a blank sheet of paper – the famous *tabula rasa* – on which experience will write.

Locke's appeal to common sense and clear thinking based on observation gained a large following that endures to this day. He said that description is the first task of philosophy. By arguing that what can be known is restricted to that which the senses can perceive he rejected any lingering traces of Neoplatonism in philosophy, along with its semi-mystical undertones. Locke developed a no-nonsense approach that described knowledge (ideas) as the aggregate of things that are given to our senses. His most influential work is *An Essay Concerning Human Understanding* (1690).

Since it is the Understanding that sets Man above the rest of sensible Beings, and gives him all the Advantage and Dominion, which he has over them; it is certainly a Subject, even for its Nobleness, worth our Labour to enquire into. The Understanding, like the Eye, whilst it makes us see, and perceive all other Things, takes no notice of it self: And it requires Art and Pains to set it at a distance, and make it its own Object.

John Locke, *An Essay Concerning Human Understanding* (1690)

As a political philosopher Locke laid out his ideas in *Two Treatises of Government* (1689). In the *First Treatise* he rejected the principle of the divine right of kings. In the *Second Treatise* he explored the distinctions between paternal, political and despotic power, and offered a liberal view of what a legitimate civil government should be. Locke is often called the 'father of liberalism' for concluding that governance should be by the consent of the governed. (This political ethic led him to take an abolitionist view against slavery.) Locke cites three abuses that can render a legitimate civil government illegitimate: unjust foreign conquest; internal usurpation of political rule; and tyrannical extension of power by those who were originally legitimately in power. When these conditions arise, he argues, revolution is a legitimate response

– even to the point of regicide (as had happened in the English Civil War of the 1640s and would happen in the French Revolution). The civil government that violates the rights of its subjects makes slaves of them, and puts itself in a state of war with them. Citizens who rise up against such a government, says Locke, are justified in so doing.

The French Enlightenment

Locke's ideas were influential in France, where the Enlightenment would reach its full vigour and launch many projects of consequence. A key thinker of the French Enlightenment was Denis Diderot (1713–84), editor of the *Encyclopédie* (1751–72), the first encyclopedia to include articles signed by its contributors. François-Marie Arouet, better known by his *nom de plume* Voltaire (1694–1778), published in virtually every genre available. His satirical novella *Candide* (1759) ridiculed Leibniz's view that we live in the 'best of all possible worlds', offering the devastating earthquake and tsunami of 1755 that destroyed most of Lisbon as a counter-example. Charles-Louis de Secondat, baron de La Brède et de Montesquieu (1689–1755), popularly known as Montesquieu, added to the political ideas of the Enlightenment the concept of the separation of powers. The ancient Greeks had devised the separation of the executive, legislative and judicial branches of government so that no single branch could control government. Montesquieu proposed the idea as a basis for modern governance, and it was adopted by the Founding Fathers of the United States of America and enshrined in the US Constitution in 1787 (a document that also owed much to the liberalism of John Locke).

The *Encyclopédie* began life as a translation of the *Cyclopaedia* (1728) by the Englishman Ephraim Chambers (*c.*1680–1740), but it evolved into something entirely different when, after a series of mishaps, the publishers gave it to Diderot, who spent the next twenty-five years compiling a book that he hoped would, as he wrote in the introduction, 'change the way people think'. It did change the way people thought, and the way in which it achieved that change was in itself change-making.

First, the contributors themselves were at the cutting edge of modern thought. They included the philosopher Étienne Bonnot de Condillac (1715–80), Montesquieu, Jean-Jacques Rousseau and Voltaire. Another modern aspect of the *Encyclopédie* was the scale of its conception and the nature of its distribution. Diderot's purpose in gathering such a distinguished band of collaborators to assist in editing the *Encyclopédie* was to create a long-lasting group of intellectuals that he called *une société des gens de lettres*, an assemblage of thinkers who comprised the new 'lettered class' which had resulted from the influence of humanism, the rise of the printing press and the availability of texts in native tongues. (Eighty-five years after Diderot's death, a group of French writers led by Honoré de Balzac [1799–1850] founded a group called the Société des Gens de Lettres, which still exists today.) In addition to gathering the best contributors and creating the idea of a 'group' (think of London's twentieth-century Bloomsbury Group or the people gathered around Jean-Paul Sartre at *Les Temps Modernes* in the 1940s, and the *Tel Quel* group, founded by Philippe Sollers [*b*.1936]), Diderot's plan was to cover all that was known to man by reason, subtitling his work a *Universal Dictionary of Arts and Sciences*. Its extent was seventeen volumes of articles and a further eleven volumes of illustrations. The twenty-eight volumes comprised twenty million words and the *Encyclopédie* had a print run of 4,250 copies. This is an astonishing figure, for single-volume books at that time rarely had print runs approaching even a thousand copies. Diderot's work was widely disseminated and its influence upon European society – and not least upon the makers of the French Revolution – cannot be overstated.

The thinker who perhaps best embodies the French Enlightenment is Voltaire. His earliest book is *Letters on the English* (1734), composed during a three-year exile in England after having made an enemy of a nobleman, who issued a *lettre de cachet* ordering Voltaire to be imprisoned indefinitely in the Bastille. (These letters – used by the nobility to condemn their social inferiors to prison – would be one cause of the French Revolution.) In England Voltaire acquainted himself with the thought of Locke and Newton. He became a champion of English empiricism, and by introducing those ideas in France he helped to end the influence of Descartes. He was also instrumental in bringing the work of William Shakespeare to the attention of a French audience.

Already liberal in outlook, Voltaire admired the freedoms enjoyed by British subjects under its constitutional monarchy. The British accommodation between Crown and parliament appeared to Voltaire in stark contrast to the absolute monarchy of his own country, where the king had unlimited power. Shakespeare was interesting to Voltaire not only because of his superior literary abilities and the sheer entertainment value of the plays, but also because he incorporated serious discussions of the roles of rulers and subjects in a way that captured the imagination of ordinary people.

. . . it must be agreed that all men being born equal, violence and ability made the first masters, the laws the most recent.

Voltaire, *Philosophical Dictionary* (1764)

(trans. Theodore Besterman, 1972)

Hume: the most important philosopher to write in English

Locke's position was amplified by the Scotsman David Hume, 'arguably, the most important philosopher ever to have written in English', according to the editors of the *Cambridge Companion to Hume* (1994). Certainly there is no area of philosophical thought not touched upon by Hume, who, modestly, considered himself a literary man first and foremost. 'Never literary attempt was more unfortunate than my *Treatise of Human Nature* (1739–40),' he wrote in *My Own Life* (1778). 'It fell *dead-born from the press*, without reaching such distinction, as even to excite a murmur among the zealots.' In time, analytic philosophy would remove itself from the realm of literary endeavour – and more's the pity, one feels, when reading Hume.

I was, I say, a man of mild disposition, of command of temper, of an open, social, and cheerful humour, capable of attachment, but little susceptible of enmity, and of great moderation in all my passions. Even my love of literary fame, my ruling passion, never soured my temper, notwithstanding my frequent disappointments.

David Hume, *My Own Life* (1778)

Hume was a sceptic who decried the influence of religion on philosophy. In *The Natural History of Religion* (1757) he argued that polytheism was humankind's natural religious tendency, and that monotheism created rigid systems that led to intolerance and, ultimately, the corruption of philosophy (when used to defend religion). Reason is not God-given. Hume saw reason as something we hold in common with the higher mammals, but considered the human variety to be superior because we have language. He was the first to outline the position of associationism, which includes the role of imagination and the passions in the formation of beliefs and ideas, which take hold by virtue of their associations in thought.

Philosophers had spent nearly 2,000 years trying to figure out how we know things. Hume, however – proving the mantra of William of Ockham that the simplest explanation is probably the best – pointed out that repetition reinforced beliefs and passions, and led us to understand how and why things work. Causal necessity largely derives from the intuition that if a + b = c in the past, it probably will in the future, giving us a predictive capability.

With Hume we see philosophy going into overdrive. Plato and Aristotle created great edifices of thought in the absence of scientific equipment with which to observe the natural phenomena they studied, and the Schoolmen built breathtaking logical confections in their attempts to reconcile reason and revelation. But in Hume we find an intelligence that is at once specific and general, scientific and metaphysical, literary and logical, and which, by comparison, makes much of today's philosophy resemble mere tinkering at the margins of the technical.

Hume's work was a great germinating force, sparking the imaginations of the best thinkers who would follow. After reading Hume's *Treatise of Human Nature*, Jeremy Bentham (1748–1832) wrote, 'I felt as if scales had fallen from my eyes. I then learned for the first time to call the cause of the people the cause of virtue' (*Fragment on Government*, 1776).

... abstruse philosophy, being founded upon a turn of mind, which cannot enter into business and action, vanishes when the philosopher leaves the shade, and comes into open day; nor can its principles easily retain any influence over our conduct and behaviour.

David Hume, *An Enquiry Concerning Human Understanding* (1748)

The German Enlightenment

The Enlightenment took a different form altogether in German-speaking Europe. The fragmented nature of pre-unification Germany meant that there was not the same sense of national identity as in France. And while the French were tired of kings, German-speakers seemed more comfortable with authoritarian rule. On the other hand, it was precisely the situation of Germany's fragmented, pre-national boundaries that gave the Enlightenment its peculiarly *German* nature. Just as the Italian language helped to create a national identity during the Italian Renaissance, so the development of German as a philosophical and literary language – and, from the eighteenth until the early twentieth centuries, as *the* mother tongue of philosophy – helped define German nationalism, and hasten unification (1871).

Christian Wolff (1679–1754), a mathematician and philosopher who was an important thinker on economics and public administration, did more than anyone to make German the language of philosophy. With him, the tradition of writing philosophy in Latin comes to a decisive halt. Wolff was a great popularizer of thought, and lectured regularly to audiences outside the University of Halle. His career as a lecturer was so successful that he died a wealthy man. The Enlightenment Germans would appear to have been thirsty for philosophy.

The playwright, poet, critic and philosopher Gotthold Ephraim Lessing (1729–81) argued for a neoclassicism that would return to Aristotelian values – an idea that helped spark Germans' comparison of their race and culture with ancient Greece. Lessing's plays often have self-explanatory titles: *The Young Scholar* (1748), *The Freethinker* (1749), *The Jews* (1749), *The Education of Humankind* (1780). *The Jews* was a typical German Enlightenment attempt to argue for the 'good Jew', and *Nathan the Wise* (1779) gave an example in a character modelled on Lessing's close friend, the Jewish-German philosopher Moses Mendelssohn (1729–86). Mendelssohn is called the father of the Haskalah or Jewish Enlightenment, and of Reform Judaism. In 1750 Frederick the Great (1712–86) gave him the status of 'Jew under extraordinary protection' (but not a citizen). His work includes *Jerusalem, or On Religious Power* (1783), which argued that religions should encourage belief through reason rather than coercion.

Like Catherine the Great in Russia, the king of Prussia Frederick the Great was a benevolent despot and a friend of learning, who attracted thinkers and writers to his court. A talented musician and composer, he once played a piano theme for the German composer Johann Sebastian Bach (1685–1750), challenging him to make a fugue of it – the result was *The Musical Offering* (BMW 1079). Frederick, who spoke all of the main European languages, kept in touch with the leading philosophers and writers of the day. He admired Voltaire, with whom he had a lengthy correspondence, and Voltaire was Frederick's guest in the royal palace from 1750 until 1753. Although Germany produced many of the greatest writers and philosophers of the period, Frederick was more enamoured of the French tradition.

The legacy of the Enlightenment

Europe's most celebrated living philosopher, Jürgen Habermas (*b*.1929), talks of an Enlightenment *project*, its aim being to describe the ongoing activities of man in a public sphere, including government, the press, the universities and, nowadays, cyberspace. But the Enlightenment was never a set of events that could be easily pinned down, and a programmatic attempt to keep the Enlightenment going as a 'project' might not be in the spirit of the Enlightenment itself. The British historian Roy Porter (1946–2002) probably had it right when he spoke of an Enlightenment *tendency*. He cites, for instance, the creation of a public space for debate in the shape of the English coffee houses, where men gathered to discuss – and influence – current affairs. The twentieth-century German-American political philosopher Hannah Arendt points out that this tendency to create a public space – wherever people may choose to gather – is a political urge that first expressed itself in ancient Greece and is further refined in the post-Enlightenment as more people are free to assemble.

The Enlightenment found its culmination in the work of Immanuel Kant (1724–1804), whose ideas mark the starting point of modern philosophy. In Kant we discover a vigorous yet refined approach to all of the epistemological, mathematical, scientific, ontological and aesthetic questions that philosophers had studied. But the issue that most exercised Kant was the problem of human freedom; and as his legacy matured in the nineteenth and twentieth centuries, the nature and limits of human freedom would be tested as never before.

PART FOUR

The Landscape of Modernity

late 18th century to early 21st century

Immanuel Kant stands at the beginning of a period in history that would open up the study of philosophy, science and literature to anyone who could read. It gave literate persons of any social station and, increasingly, ethnicity or religion, the wherewithal to contribute to public debate by writing and publishing. And it is not merely the democratization of thought that is revolutionary: it is also the nature of the ideas.

Ancient Greek philosophy inquired widely into the state of human existence and the world we inhabit. It asked enduring questions and offered answers, many of which are relevant to philosophy today. The supplanting of Greek thought by Christian ideas led to more than 1,500 years of rhetorical flourish and ingenious logic, but it severely inhibited philosophical and scientific inquiry by demanding that God be the starting point and end point of any investigation. The Scientific Revolution and the rise of humanism during the Renaissance increasingly put man at the centre of philosophical inquiry. Kant finally reversed the long reign of Scholastic thinking. Increasingly, the beginning and the end of philosophical investigation would be mankind; our thoughts were free to go wherever they desired.

Immanuel Kant

If, as Alfred North Whitehead observed, the European philosophical tradition consists of a series of footnotes to Plato, then the modern period might be more accurately described as a series of footnotes to Kant. Plato raised the big questions of philosophy, and Aristotle created the first philosophical system, but Kant is the first great system-builder of the modern period, taking into account the impact of the Scientific Revolution and the Enlightenment.

> . . . all thought, whether straightaway (*directe*) or through a detour (*indirecte*), must ultimately be related to intuitions, thus, in our case, to sensibility, since there is no other way in which objects can be given to us.
>
> Immanuel Kant, *Critique of Pure Reason* (1781)
> (trans. by Paul Guyer and Allen W. Wood, 1998)

For Kant, philosophy is about man having reached the age of intellectual maturity, when the universe can be explained by thought rather than revelation. He was profoundly influenced by David Hume, whom he credits with awakening him from a 'dogmatic slumber'. In his *Prolegomena to Any Future Metaphysics* (1783) Kant said that, after reading Hume, 'I could proceed safely, though slowly, to determine the whole sphere of pure reason completely and from general principles, in its circumference as well as in its contents. This was required for metaphysics in order to construct its system according to a reliable plan.' This groundwork led to Kant's masterpiece, *The Critique of Pure Reason* (1781, substantially revised in 1787).

> Morality began with the noblest attribute of human nature, the development and cultivation of which give a prospect of infinite utility; and ended in fanaticism or superstition.
>
> Immanuel Kant, *Critique of Practical Reason* (1788)
> (trans. Thomas Kingsmill Abbott, 1889)

Inspired by Enlightenment thinking about freedom – and experiencing the effects of war first-hand when his hometown of Königsberg was under Russian occupation during the Seven Years' War (1756–63) – Kant argued that knowledge and freedom went hand in hand. He explored these themes in two further critiques: the *Critique of Practical Reason* (1788) and the *Critique of Judgement* (1790). The *Critique of Pure Reason* identifies laws that govern science, while preserving free will. The *Critique of Judgement* considers aesthetic judgements, and teleological questions about the purpose of natural organisms and systems.

One of the most enduring aspects of Kant's philosophy is his ethics, with its categorical imperative. The categorical imperative says that I must act in such a way that the action I am choosing should become a universal law that should be applied to anyone else finding themselves in similar circumstances. Here Kant argues against a consequentialist ethics like utilitarianism. Utilitarian ethics say the right course of action is that which gives the greatest amount of good to the greatest number of people. Utilitarianism is consequentialist because it urges me to seek the best conse-quences, which, Kant argues, is no more than my animal self would do. For Kant utilitarianism is not a moral theory because it does not take sufficient account of the difference between animals and persons, i.e., mind. In seeking the categorical imperative for our actions, we are using what Kant calls pure practical reason to arrive at a maxim that would govern our actions. This is called deontological ethics: finding and observing a moral rule, rather than defining good by its consequences.

Kant's *transcendental idealism*, in which the perceiving subject partly assigns meaning to the external world, was highly influential.

Essentially, various forms of idealism would characterize German thought for the next two centuries. Initially, idealism was slow to take on in England, though the Irish cleric George Berkeley (1685–1753) believed that the external world was made up of ideas. The great English author and lexicographer Samuel Johnson (1709–84), whose *A Dictionary of the English Language* was published in 1755, disagreed with Bishop Berkeley's idealism. He kicked a large stone and proclaimed: 'I refute it thus!'

The improvement of man

The moral and social perfectibility of man preoccupied thinkers in the early modern period. How could philosophy help? The Swiss philosopher and writer Jean-Jacques Rousseau (1712–78), whose most enduring work is *The Social Contract, or Principles of Political Right* (1762), believed that man was by nature *good*, but was corrupted by society. In *The Social Contract* he famously declared, 'Man is born free, and everywhere he is in chains.'

Rousseau's idea of a social contract between the governing and the governed followed from his *Discourse on the Origin and Basis of Inequality among Men* (1754) and his *Discourse on Political Economy* (1755). Rousseau elaborated a version of popular sovereignty that defines political legislation as acts of the 'general will', which applies to all citizens equally, because it derives from all citizens alike. (Such thinking would later offer the ideologues behind the French Revolution a justification for their radical actions.) Following in the new tradition of philosopher-novelists like Voltaire, Rousseau published *Julie, or the New Héloïse* (1761), which explored the issues of human freedom raised by the love affair of Abélard and Héloïse (see p.75). Rousseau considered his most important book to be *Émile, or On Education* (1762), which was extremely influential in shaping the French educational system after the Revolution.

> I mean to inquire if, in the civil order, there can be any sure and legitimate rule of administration, men being taken as they are and laws as they might be. In this inquiry I shall endeavour always to unite what right sanctions with what is prescribed by interest, in order that justice and utility may in no case be divided.
>
> Jean-Jacques Rousseau, *The Social Contract* (1762)
> (trans. G. D. H. Cole, 1923)

A consequence of this new emphasis on the self and the individual is that ordinary people began to recognize themselves more as free, independent beings, rather than as subjects of a king or queen. This Enlightenment ideal is best expressed in the opening words of the United States' Declaration of Independence (1776) written by Thomas Jefferson (1743–1826): 'We hold these truths to be self-evident, that all men are created equal, that they are endowed by their Creator with certain unalienable Rights, that among these are Life, Liberty, and the Pursuit of Happiness. That to secure these rights, Governments are instituted among Men, deriving their just powers from the consent of the governed.' The American Revolution (1775–83) and the French Revolution (1789) were not merely the uprisings of disenfranchised subjects who rejected monarchy: they were the products of Enlightenment philosophy, disseminated through popular pamphlets offering intellectual justification or criticism of political action. Notable among these pamphleteers were the Anglo-Irishman Edmund Burke (1729–97) and the Englishman Thomas Paine (1737–1809).

Burke trained in the law, but had a keen philosophical mind. While he is best known for his pamphlets in support of the American cause – *American Taxation* (1774) and *Conciliation with America* (1775) – his ability to make informed judgements in practical politics and political theory was a result of years of philosophical study. In an early work, *A Philosophical Enquiry into the Origin of our Ideas of the Sublime and Beautiful* (1757), he argued that reason allows us to recognize beauty, because it enables us to make judgements about the beautiful. In Burke, we see how a theory of perception can inform political theory – a persuasive argument for the practical value of philosophy. Thomas Paine's pamphlets in support of the American Revolution include *Common Sense* and

The Crisis, both published in 1776. Burke and Paine were on opposite sides of the debate surrounding the French Revolution. Paine's
pro-Revolution *Rights of Man* (1791) answered Burke's *Reflections
on the Revolution in France* (1790). In this period ideas were not
only developed by philosophers, they were put into action by a
new public hungry to think and act for themselves.

In England, the philosopher and jurist Jeremy Bentham and
the Scottish-born philosopher James Mill (1773–1836) developed
the doctrine of utilitarianism, which defines the right act as that
which gives the greatest amount of good to the greatest number
of people. From our vantage point in the twenty-first century,
Bentham appears to be not only a modern thinker, but a contemporary one. He argued in favour of the rights of animals, was an
early theorist of the welfare state, recommended the decriminal-
ization of homosexual acts, and was an advocate of the separation of church and state, and of divorce, while he opposed slavery
and the death penalty. Bentham also invented the panopticon, a
prison design in which inmates are under surveillance at all times
without being able to see who is observing them.

A less optimistic English thinker of the time was Thomas
Malthus (1766–1834), an ordained minister, political economist
and demographer whose present-day reputation rests upon *An
Essay on the Principle of Population* (1798–1826). Unlike Rousseau,
Malthus did not think that humankind was perfectible. He believed

that population growth was the enemy of human perfection. He argued that the planet lacked the capacity to provide for an endlessly expanding population, and that civilization would suffer as a result (ultimately, the poor were to blame for this). Later reformers would use Malthus's predictions to make the argument for limiting population growth, either through discouragement or active intervention using compulsory sterilization.

Absolute idealism

We have said that Kant is the father of modern philosophy, and no other philosopher fell so completely under his spell as his fellow German Johann Gottlieb Fichte (1762–1814). Fichte further systematized Kant's transcendental idealism to form what he called *Wissenschaftslehre* or 'Doctrine of Scientific Knowledge', a new approach that he believed could give an account of everything – the sciences, law, ethics, and even the philosophy of religion.

> Our own consciousness is the source of all our positive and certain knowledge. It precedes, and is the ground of, all other knowledge; nay it embraces within itself everything which we truly *know*.
>
> J. G. Fichte, *Memoir* (1848–9)
> (trans. William Smith, 1848–9)

Fichte took human subjectivity – the 'I' – to a new level in philosophy, way past what Augustine or Descartes could have imagined. He called it 'the pure I'. But in Fichte there is no hint of solipsism, the position that only one's self and one's experiences exist. Just as I am conscious of myself, he argued in the *Foundations of Natural Right* (1796), I am also conscious of other subjectivities, other 'I's. This is an important moment in modern philosophy, because it will inform all discussion that follows (at least in the continental tradition) of the relations of self and others. Fichte is saying that my awareness of my self and the selves of others is the basis for *intersubjectivity*: the mutual acknowledgement of selves that is the opposite of solipsism and brings about our social world. Fichte conceives the 'I' not as an abstract absolute, but rather as an embodied presence in the world.

Fichte did not confine himself to the rarified air of pure subjectivity. He was a popular orator in Germany when it was under French occupation by Napoleon's troops, following the Prussian defeat at Jena (1806). In 1808 he delivered a series of *Addresses to the German Nation* which were a significant influence on the emerging sensibility of German nationalism. Fichte rooted his sense of Germanness in the German language, which he viewed as having classical antecedents, and argued that German patriots should stand against the French. Fichte was also an anti-Semite who argued that the extension of German citizenship to Jews would weaken the nation.

Fichte's successor in the development of German idealism is Friedrich W. J. Schelling (1775–1854), whose *System of Transcendental Idealism* (1800) outlines his project to create a philosophy of nature and to deduce an objective system of reason. Fichte characterized nature as the 'I' (mind) in the process of becoming. While Schelling's *Naturphilosophie* has not endured into the twenty-first century, it was a major influence on philosophers of the twentieth century, including Heidegger, the German-American existentialist theologian Paul Tillich (1886–1965), and the French thinkers Derrida and Jacques Lacan (1901–81). His main contribution to their work was his challenge to the Cartesian view of the 'I' as being transparent to itself. Schelling sensed that the 'I' is a more complicated and obscure construction.

> The task of establishing a science of knowledge, a science which puts the subjective first and foremost, immediately compels one towards a highest principle of all knowledge.
>
> Friedrich W. J. Schelling, *System of Transcendental Idealism* (1800) (trans. Peter L. Heath, 1997)

Schelling rejected all attempts to understand the world by reductive means or by mechanical analogy. In this, Schelling is the philosopher who best echoes the preoccupations of German Romanticism, a paradoxical 'movement' in that it flourishes in the context of Kantian idealism (which is rational and rigorous), yet at the same time rejects rationality in favour of the irrational creative fire of 'genius' and the untameable power of nature. The polymathic writer and philosopher-scientist Johann Wolfgang von Goethe (1749–1832) epitomized this struggle in his verse drama *Faust* (1808, 1832), in which the wandering conjuror Faust has reached the end of his empirical researches and longs for more – for an explanation of everything that can be known, for transcendental knowledge. He sells his soul to the devil and this 'Faustian pact' comes to symbolize both the extraordinary discoveries of empiricism and their limitations. Faust wants more than pure science can supply.

The philosophical contradictions of German Romanticism, which flourished in the late eighteenth and early nineteenth centuries, led the German philosopher Friedrich Nietzsche (1844–1900) to describe this phenomenon as the *Gegenaufklärung* or 'anti-Enlightenment'.

Hegel and the climax of German idealism

Immanuel Kant's legacy of idealist systems – and indeed the Enlightenment itself – reaches its apotheosis in the work of

G. W. F. Hegel (1770–1831). Like Kant and Fichte, Hegel sought to create a system that would explain everything. His main works are: *Phenomenology of Spirit* (1807), *Science of Logic* (1812–16), *Encyclopedia of the Philosophical Sciences* (1817, 1827) and *Philosophy of Right* (1820).

In his phenomenology of mind Hegel dismisses the epistemologies of Enlightenment thinkers from Descartes to Kant, because of their foundationalism (their desire to find a firm base upon which to build their knowledge). Hegel's focus is not just on consciousness and its objects: the subject of his phenomenology of mind is *consciousness being conscious of having objects*. Hegel's method is dialectical, which is to say that it proceeds by describing a *thesis*, which is contradicted by an *antithesis*; these opposing positions yield a *synthesis*, and the whole process begins anew. His work is very challenging to read.

> Because philosophy has its being essentially in the element of that universality which encloses the particular within it, the end or final result seems, in the case of philosophy more than in that of other sciences, to have absolutely expressed the complete fact itself in its very nature.
>
> G. W. F. Hegel, *Phenomenology of Spirit* (1807)
> (trans. A. V. Miller, 1977)

Hegel intended the *Phenomenology* as a prelude to his *Science of Logic*, which does not treat logic in a traditional, Aristotelian way. Having argued in the *Phenomenology* that what we call reality is so influenced by our perception of it that, ultimately, it *is* mind, in the *Logic* Hegel shows how everything in the world can be explained by the underlying order that consciousness makes of reality. This order *is* logic; so the science of logic, for Hegel, is an attempt to understand the underlying structure of the world we make.

After dealing with mind and logic, Hegel undertook the larger issues of ethics, politics and the law in *Elements of the Philosophy of Right*. Hegel believed that law was of primary importance to the organization of a society that wished to avoid despotism, and he viewed human freedom as only realizing itself through participation in civic and social life. He identified three spheres in which 'right' operates: *abstract right*, *morality* and *ethicality*. Abstract right concerns our relations with others, and outlines the basic principle of 'non-interference' to describe how we should respect the rights of others (and what we expect in return). Morality involves our understanding of our own subjectivity (or 'particularity'), as outlined in the *Phenomenology*, as the basis upon which we can acknowledge the subjectivity of others, and therefore respect their rights as if they *were* us. Morality concerns the problems of purpose and responsibility; intention and well-being; and 'the good' and conscience. In the third sphere, 'ethicality', Hegel synthesizes the subjective experience of the individual with the progressively larger groups in which he or she exists: the family, civil society, the state.

In the twenty-first century Hegel is remembered less for his ethical, political and legal ruminations than for his historicism, which would inspire the German political philosopher Karl Marx (1818–83). Hegel argued that all societies and the activities that take place in them, from art to science to politics, are defined by their history, which is the key to understanding them. From a Marxist perspective, if one changes elements in society – altering the domination of one class by another, changing the relationship of labour to capital – then one can change the course of history by creating another, more desirable outcome. From 1830 to 1831 Hegel gave a series of lectures on *The Philosophy of History* (1837), which argued that history is determined by God. Marx would turn Hegel's philosophy of history on its head, replacing God with class struggle. In *The Open Society and Its Enemies* (1945) Karl Popper said that Hegel, along with Plato and Marx, was a fore-father of totalitarianism.

Schopenhauer and the limits of rationality

Where Hegel was a daunting and opaque prose stylist, the German philosopher Arthur Schopenhauer (1788–1860) wrote in a clear, engaging and entertaining way that is unusual in the philosophy of the period. He was a master of the aphorism (from the Greek, meaning 'distinction' or 'definition'), a brief statement that offers a condensed view or judgement. A good example would be Schopenhauer's observation that 'obscurity and vagueness of expression is always and everywhere a bad sign: for in ninety-nine cases out of a hundred it derives from vagueness of thought, which in turn comes from an original incongruity and inconsistency in the thought itself, and thus from its falsity' (*Parerga and Paralipomena*, 1851). In the twentieth century Schopenhauer was characterized as a pessimist whose importance lay in his influence on Friedrich Nietzsche, rather than as a philosopher worthy of study in his own right. His key work is *The World as Will and Representation* (1818) in which the will is presented as an 'aimless desire to perpetuate itself'.

A man who tries to live on the generosity of the Muses, I mean on his poetic gifts, seems to me somewhat to resemble a girl who lives on her charms. Both profane for base profit what ought to be the free gift of their innermost being.

Arthur Schopenhauer, *Parerga and Paralipomena* (1851)

(trans. E. F. J. Payne, 1974)

Schopenhauer describes man as driven by physical and sexual desires that ultimately cannot be fulfilled. He argues for the negation of desire as a road to happiness, and in this his thought has much in common with Buddhism. Schopenhauer is rare among German philosophers in searching out Eastern influences: he read the Hindu *Upanishads* daily, and also practised meditation. In the end, Schopenhauer is more ironist than pessimist. To those with the requisite turn of mind, he is a delightful companion on life's occasionally rocky road.

Karl Marx and the legacy of Hegel

Ludwig Andreas Feuerbach (1804–72) was one of a new group of left-wing German philosophers known as the Young Hegelians, to which Karl Marx and his collaborator Friedrich Engels (1820–95) belonged. Feuerbach's *The Essence of Christianity* (1841) argued that Christianity was a man-created myth, and that God existed only as a projection of humankind's need for him, a process which led man to be alienated from himself, compromising his own autonomy. This is the source of Marx's famous remark, in his 1844 essay 'A Contribution to the Critique of Hegel's Philosophy of Right', that religion is the 'opium of the people'. For Feuerbach, man was himself divine. The main argument of *The Essence of Christianity* is that man has the ability to create himself and determine his place in the universe. Feuerbach's book introduced post-Hegelian ideas to a popular audience in England through the 1854 translation by Mary Ann Evans (1819–80), who also wrote novels under the pseudonym George Eliot.

> The materialist doctrine that men are products of circum-stances and upbringing, and that, therefore, changed men are products of changed circumstances and changed up-bringing, forgets that it is men who change circumstances and that the educator must himself be educated. Hence this doctrine is bound to divide society into two parts, one of which is superior to society. The coincidence of the changing of circumstances and of human activity or self-change [*Selbstveränderung*] can be conceived and rationally under-stood only as revolutionary practice.
>
> Karl Marx, 'Theses on Feuerbach' (1845)
>
> (trans. W. Lough, 1969)

Socialism was not yet a coherent doctrine in the first half of the nineteenth century. The term was coined by the Frenchman Count Henri de Saint-Simon (1760–1825), who believed that science and technology would be harnessed to provide a fairer society based on equality of opportunity. His compatriot Pierre Leroux (1797–1871) argued for the absolute equality of men, while Marie Roch Louis Reybaud (1799–1879) published the first history of socialism, *Études sur les Reformateurs ou Socialistes Modernes* (*Studies on the Reformers or Modern Socialists*, 1840). Another important early socialist was the Welshman Robert Owen (1771–1858), the father of the cooperative movement. Marx's achievement was to weave these disparate strands into a coherent theory that provided a foundation for political action.

Marx's most popular work is *The Communist Manifesto* (1848), co-written with Engels. His most important is *Das Kapital* (1867), a detailed description of the relations between capital and labour. From an intellectual standpoint, Marx's great achievement was to combine politics, philosophy and economics into a method that provided tools for people to analyse their situation (and, if they wished, to change it through revolutionary action).

The history of all hitherto existing society is the history of class struggles.

> Karl Marx and Friedrich Engels, *The Communist Manifesto* (1848) (trans. Samuel Moore, 1888)

Søren Kierkegaard: the first existentialist

While Hegel and Marx looked at man in relation to his historical position, the Danish philosopher Søren Kierkegaard (1813–55) was more concerned with his individual existence. Kierkegaard is, par excellence, the philosopher of subjectivity. An early crisis in his life – the breaking off of his engagement to Regine Olsen – resulted in a flurry of three books published in 1843, whose titles suggest the agenda for the existential philosophy he helped to create: *Either-Or*, *Fear and Trembling* and *Repetition*. In the next three years he published *Philosophical Fragments* (1844), *The Concept of Anxiety* (1844), *Stages on Life's Way* (1845) and his *Concluding Unscientific Postscript* (1846). Two posthumous works continue to have an influence in the twenty-first century: *The Sickness unto Death* (1849) and *Training in Christianity* (1850). When it comes to finding original titles for philosophy books, Kierkegaard is the undisputed champion of all time.

Kierkegaard viewed man as being free to choose *himself*. That choice is the essence of human freedom. Being conscious of existence, of freedom, is challenging; but the failure to be conscious of oneself and the possibilities for freedom leads to despair. (Hence existentialism's largely deserved reputation for gloom.) However, recognizing despair presents the opportunity to *be* oneself. In *The Sickness unto Death* Kierkegaard writes: 'Despair is a sickness in the spirit, in the self, and so it may assume a triple form: in despair at not being conscious of having a self (despair improperly so called); in despair at not willing to be oneself; in despair at willing to be oneself.'

Kierkegaard was the first modern philosopher to recognize embodiment as a key to understanding human subjectivity. We are all embodied, and we perceive the world and act in it from a location in space and time – in other words, from a perspective. Kierkegaard's philosophy is at odds with that of Hegel or other systematizers who believe they can achieve the God-like perspective of a completely 'objective' science. This claim, says Kierkegaard, is doomed to pseudo-objectivity and error. The purpose of man is, Kierkegaard believed, to find himself in religious faith, which he viewed as a kind of supra-rational understanding that required an enormous effort on his part: the famous leap of faith (or 'leap to faith', as Kierkegaard originally put it).

Christianity has discovered an evil which man as such does not know of; this misery is the sickness unto death.

Søren Kierkegaard, *The Sickness unto Death* (1849)

(trans. Edna H. Hong and Howard V. Hong, 1941)

Emerson and Thoreau: the first American philosophers

American philosophy begins with Ralph Waldo Emerson (1803–82) and Henry David Thoreau (1817–62). Both men belonged to the Transcendentalist movement, which rejected the doctrine of Unitarianism associated with Harvard University's School of Divinity.

The Transcendentalists believed that spirituality was arrived at by intuition, rather than through church doctrine and intellectual effort. They were particularly concerned with the theme of nature, and Emerson is best known for his essay *Nature* (1836).

> The stars awaken a certain reverence, because though always present, they are inaccessible; but all natural objects make a kindred impression, when the mind is open to their influence. Nature never wears a mean appearance. Neither does the wisest man extort her secret, and lose his curiosity by finding out all her perfection.
>
> Ralph Waldo Emerson, *Nature* (1836)

Emerson travelled to Europe in 1832 to meet the English philosopher John Stuart Mill (1806–73), and the Romantic poets William Wordsworth (1770–1850) and Samuel Taylor Coleridge (1772–1834). He also befriended the Scottish essayist Thomas Carlyle (1795–1881), author of the satirical work *Sartor Resartus* (1836) and *The French Revolution: A History* (1837). Carlyle studied German literature and translated Goethe, whose work he introduced to Emerson; in return, Emerson contributed an introduction to *Sartor Resartus*, and became Carlyle's literary agent in the United States. The Transcendentalists admired the Kantian idealism of Wordsworth and Coleridge. They rejected Mill's empiricism, but embraced his thinking on justice. Emerson was the first American thinker to have influenced a European philosopher: Nietzsche's notebooks contain several references to his work.

Emerson mentored Thoreau, whose lasting contribution to American thought rests on two works: *Walden* (1854) and *Civil Disobedience* (1849). *Walden* is a diary of an experiment in which Thoreau 'returns to nature', building himself a small cabin and living a life of self-sufficiency in rural Massachusetts. In his reflections Thoreau makes many enduring observations on the nature of knowledge, the 'I', social and labour relations, and man's relationship with nature. *Civil Disobedience* is a famous defence of conscience that justifies the author's refusal to pay taxes because he viewed the United States' war against Mexico as an effort to expand slavery. Thoreau wrote the essay while in jail, and his example was later cited by Martin Luther King (1929–68) as the inspiration for his 'Letter from a Birmingham Jail' (1963).

That government is best which governs not at all.

Henry David Thoreau, *Civil Disobedience* (1849)

Positivism and empiricism

The subjective metaphysics of Kierkegaard and the Transcendentalism of Emerson and Thoreau were critical of science, and indicated new philosophical paths that depended more upon intuition than observation. In England, however, the British empirical tradition that began with Locke and Hume was being further developed by John Stuart Mill, while in France the philosopher Auguste Comte (1798–1857) replaced the metaphysics of Kant and Hegel with a new approach to thinking that said human knowledge could only be composed of that which was directly observable: positivism. Comte devised 'The Law of Three Stages' to explain man's evolutionary journey from a 'Theological Stage' (belief in gods or God) to an intermediate 'Metaphysical Stage' and, finally, the 'Positivist Stage'. The most enduring value of Comte's work is that it laid the groundwork for sociology.

> I believe that I have discovered a great fundamental law, to which the mind is subjected by an invariable necessity.
> Auguste Comte, *Course in Positivist Philosophy* (1830–42)
> (trans. Paul Descours and H. G. Jones, 1905)

Increasingly in the nineteenth century the social sciences were coming to occupy a place not only in philosophy, but also in the practical administration of human affairs. John Stuart Mill developed the utilitarian philosophy of his father James Mill and Jeremy Bentham into a definitive style of British empiricism that would influence liberal economic and political policy. In his political treatise *On Liberty* (1859) Mill argued for the sovereignty of the individual and against the 'tyranny of the majority'. His defence of women's rights in *The Subjection of Women* (1869), co-written with Harriet Taylor (1807–58), argued for female suffrage. He published *The Principles of Political Economy* in 1848, the year of *The Communist Manifesto* and of revolution in Europe. Mill's most enduring purely philosophical work may be *A System of Logic* (1843), the foundation of his radical empiricism, which held that the 'necessary' truths of logic and mathematics could be derived from experience.

> Men do not want solely the obedience of women, they want their sentiments. All men, except the most brutish, desire to have, in the woman most connected with them, not a forced slave but a willing one, not only a slave merely, but a favourite.
>
> John Stuart Mill, *The Subjection of Women* (1869)

Darwin and evolution

The English naturalist Charles Darwin (1809–82) is responsible not only for popularizing one of the most seductive metaphors of explanation – the idea that things evolve – but also for laying the theoretical basis for describing the origin of species, including *Homo sapiens*, and the mechanism by which they evolve: natural selection. The key work in evolutionary theory is *On the Origin of Species by Natural Selection* (1859), followed by *The Descent of Man* (1871), which argues for man's common ancestry with the animal kingdom. Darwin's evolutionary theory was as challenging to the status quo in the nineteenth century as the Copernican revolution had been in the sixteenth. The Earth (from fossil records) was shown to be many times older than the 6,000 years suggested in the Old Testament – or the precise measurement given by the seventeenth-century scholar Archbishop James Ussher (1581–1656), who had calculated the time and date of Creation as the night preceding Sunday, 23 October 4004 BC. Evolutionary theory argued that God was not the creator of mankind; mankind was now seen as the result of a biological process. This led Christians of the time to the alarming prospect that the purpose of man was no longer to perfect himself in striving towards salvation in Jesus Christ.

Darwin traced his own journey from being what he called an 'orthodox' Christian, who was sometimes laughed at for his quotation of scripture, to someone whose eyes were opened by science as he moved from belief to knowledge. As an undergraduate Darwin said he had virtually learned by heart William Paley's (1743–1805) *Natural Theology, or Evidences of the Existence and Attributes of the Deity, Collected from the Appearances of Nature* (1802). In that book Paley used the metaphor of the watchmaker to make the teleological argument from design: 'Every indication of contrivance, every manifestation of design, which existed in the watch, exists in the works of nature; with the difference, on the side of nature, of being greater or more, and that in a degree which exceeds all computation.'

> If humankind evolved by Darwinian natural selection, genetic chance and environmental necessity, not God, made the species. Deity can still be sought in the origin of the ultimate units of matter, in quarks and electron shells (Hans Küng was right to ask atheists why there is something instead of nothing) but not in the origin of species. However much we embellish that stark conclusion with metaphor and imagery, it remains the philosophical legacy of the last century of scientific research.
>
> E. O. Wilson, *On Human Nature* (1978)

To the young Darwin, the study of Paley's work 'was the only part of the academical course which, as I then felt and as I still believe, was of the least use to me in the education of my mind'. But the truths of science necessarily overwrote the beliefs of scripture for Darwin. In the end, he wrote in his autobiography, 'The mystery of the beginning of all things is insoluble to us; and I for one must be content to remain an Agnostic.' The result of

Darwin's theory was to create more, not less, work for clerics as they set out to soothe popular fears over the prospect of a godless universe. At worst they had to bring lost souls back to the flock; at best they had to revise or revive the Aristotelian argument of the unmoved mover who created the universe, but then sat back and had no further hand in man's development.

A new breed of social thinkers found in evolution a powerful metaphor for political manipulation. Herbert Spencer (1820–1903) invented the doctrine of 'social Darwinism', based on a contest in which man was pitted against man, rather like the beasts, in a struggle for the 'survival of the fittest'. In the early twentieth century those in favour of an unregulated free-market economy used this argument against the idea of a welfare state or any kind of national insurance-based initiative, such as workers' compensation or universal healthcare. The ideas of Malthus thus reinvigorated, Darwin's half-cousin Francis Galton (1822–1911) fashioned the pseudo-science of *eugenics* to 'improve the race', either by breeding from the 'fittest' or by sterilizing the 'unfit'. Eugenics was an idea that captured the imagination of such prominent figures in British public life as the writer H. G. Wells (1866–1946), the economist John Maynard Keynes (1883–1946), the social activists Sidney (1859–1947) and Beatrice Webb (1858–1943) and the politician Winston Churchill (1874–1965). Eventually, eugenics programmes would be discredited when hundreds of thousands of people were forcibly sterilized by the Nazis.

C. S. Peirce and pragmatism

The American philosopher, logician and mathematician Charles Sanders Peirce (1839–1914) is the father of pragmatism, the doctrine that propositions are true if they work, and that unpractical ideas should be rejected. Pragmatism is a uniquely American tendency, and it continues to have a distinctive impact on contemporary philosophy.

Perhaps more than any other modern thinker, Peirce's philosophy flows directly from Kant, whom he regards as his master. The two have much in common, both being polymaths with expertise in a wide number of fields. In addition to the work in logic, pragmatism and semiotics for which he is primarily known today, Peirce made lasting and practical contributions in mathematics, astronomy, chemistry, geodesy, surveying, cartography, meteorology, spectroscopy, psychology, philology, lexicography, the history of science and mathematical economy.

Peirce may be the best example of the argument that modern philosophy is a series of footnotes to Kant. He specifically followed Kant in the belief that illusion and error in thinking are most often caused by faulty inferences. In 'The Fixation of Belief'

(1877) Peirce wrote that the power of drawing inferences was the highest of all human intellectual faculties, and the last to develop. He called it 'not so much a natural gift as a long and difficult art' – and it was that art that helped Peirce develop his pragmatic method. Peirce also developed an important system of logic, and was a pioneer in semiotics. Semiotics is the science of signs that developed in a philosophical direction under the American philosopher Charles W. Morris (1901–79), whose interests lay in logical positivism and pragmatism, and in quite another direction, towards structuralism, in the work of the Swiss linguist Ferdinand de Saussure (1857–1913).

Peirce's pragmatism was the starting point for several generations of American philosophers, starting with five luminaries who were born in the nineteenth century: William James (1842–1910), Josiah Royce (1855–1916), George Herbert Mead (1863–1931), George Santayana (1863–1952) and John Dewey (1859–1952). Today, the English philosopher Susan Haack (*b*.1945) is often referred to as Peirce's intellectual granddaughter.

Pragmatism might never have survived into the twenty-first century had it not been taken up by William James, because Peirce's character was generally held in low regard by his peers, so his ideas did not gain the attention they deserved during his lifetime. James – brother of the novelist Henry James (1843–1916) – is best remembered in the twenty-first century for his *Principles of*

Psychology (1890), the first comprehensive account of the subject in English. All of James's work may be seen as examples of a pragmatic method, including *Varieties of Religious Experience* (1902) and *Essays in Radical Empiricism* (1912). James is popularly remembered for characterizing our perception of time as a 'stream of consciousness'. This discovery had a profound effect on the writing styles of his student Gertrude Stein (1874–1946), and upon the international literary scene at the beginning of the twentieth century, in France (Marcel Proust, 1871–1922), England (Virginia Woolf, 1882–1941), Ireland (James Joyce, 1882–1941), and the United States (William Faulkner, 1897–1962).

. . . a movement is a change, a process; so we see that in the time-world and the space-world alike the first known things are not elements, but combinations, not separate units, but wholes already formed. The condition of *being* of the wholes may be the elements; but the condition of our *knowing* the elements is our having already felt the wholes as wholes.

William James, *Principles of Psychology* (1890)

American pragmatism continued with John Dewey, who, after an early attachment to idealism went on to develop a programme of pragmatism that included important writings on psychology, educational reform and the democratic process. Dewey concentrated on the role of experience, which he regarded as vital. His focus on a child's experience of education led to his first text on educational reform, *The Child and the Curriculum* (1902). Dewey ran a laboratory school at the University of Chicago where he could test his theories, and this work resulted in *The School and Society* (1899) and *Moral Principles in Education* (1909). As a practical philosopher, he was a founder of the New School for Social Research in New York City (1919), Bennington College in Vermont, and the experimental Black Mountain College in North Carolina. Dewey's political theory held that freedom requires a politically active and informed electorate, ideas he explored in *The Public and Its Problems* (1927), *Liberalism and Social Action* (1935), and *Freedom and Culture* (1939).

George Santayana, also a pragmatist, could not tolerate Transcendentalism in American philosophy or Puritanism in American social mores. He was the first American philosopher to develop an original aesthetics and theory of values. His *The Sense of Beauty* (1896) is the first American work on the subject. In it, he rejects the classical tautology of 'beauty is truth, truth beauty' to demand a rigorous definition of 'the exposition of the origin, place and elements of beauty as an object of human experience'. The new role of the philosopher in aesthetics is to discover the elements of our nature that make us 'sensible to beauty'. Santayana's most radical conceptual development was his emphasis on the observer's role in constituting the aesthetic object. Santayana made other important contributions to American philosophy, including his naturalist account of the world, *Scepticism and Animal Faith: Introduction to a System of Philosophy* (1923).

> What people have respected have been rather scraps of official philosophy, or entire systems, which they have inherited or imported, as they have respected operas and art museums. To be on speaking terms with these fine things was part of a social respectability, like having family silver.
>
> George Santayana, *Character and Opinion in the United States* (1920)

Modernism via scholasticism and hermeneutics

In his doctoral thesis *On the Several Senses of Being in Aristotle* (1862) the German-Austrian philosopher Franz Brentano (1838–1916) reintroduced Aquinas's theory of *intentionality* as a key philosophical concept that would have a profound influence on his pupil Edmund Husserl and, in turn, on Husserl's students.

The German theological tradition underwent something of a renaissance in the work of Wilhelm Dilthey (1833–1911), who had studied the classical hermeneutics of Friedrich Schleiermacher (1768–1834). The term *hermeneutics* was first used to describe the critical study of biblical texts, of Talmudic interpretation (see p.44). Schleiermacher developed hermeneutics as a tool for the analysis of larger 'texts', including groups or societies. For Schleiermacher, textual interpretation requires knowledge of the historical context in which a text was written, along with information about the biography and worldview of the author. Dilthey further stressed the central importance of biography in developing his new method for the study of society and culture, which he termed *Verstehen* ('to understand').

German philosophy took an unusual turn in 1872 when Friedrich Nietzsche published *The Birth of Tragedy*, which contrasts the Apollonian and Dionysian impulses in ancient Greece. Nietzsche's highly original observation was to identify as the motor of Greek tragedy tensions between the Dionysian or irrational creative life force, and the Appollonian impulse towards order. Unlike his colleagues, Nietzsche was trained as a philologist, not a philosopher. He developed an aphoristic writing style and an ironic stance that made him the most popular – and most controversial – of modern German philosophers.

Nietzsche is notorious for declaring the 'death of God' in *The Gay Science* (1882). The challenge for modern man, he argued, was to take responsibility for his life through striving and will. Influenced by Schopenhauer's *The World as Will and Representation*, Nietzsche coined the term *will to power* to describe the life force that drives human existence. After the death of God, Nietzsche claimed, man needed a *revaluing of all values*. Among his other influential ideas are the concept of the *eternal return* (we should live each moment as if it will recur endlessly) and the 'overman' (*Übermensch*), a higher state of being attained by exercising the will to power. Nietzsche's key works include *The Gay Science*, *Beyond Good and Evil* (1886), *On the Genealogy of Morals* (1887) and *Thus Spake Zarusthustra* (1883–85).

> The Christian concept of a god – the god as the patron of the sick, the god as a spinner of cobwebs, the god as a spirit – is one of the most corrupt concepts that has ever been set up in the world: it probably touches the low-water mark in the ebbing evolution of the god-type. God degenerated into the contradiction of life. Instead of being its transfiguration and eternal Yea! In him war is declared on life, on nature, on the will to live!
>
> Friedrich Nietzsche, *The Anti-Christ* (1888)
> (trans. H. L. Mencken, 1918)

Gottlob Frege and the birth of logicism

The German mathematician Gottlob Frege (1848–1925) was an obscure figure until Bertrand Russell (1872–1970) drew attention to his work in arithmetic and logic, which would lay the foundations of analytic philosophy. Analytic philosophy has been the dominant force in Anglo-American philosophy since the early twentieth century. It reduces problems to their component parts, discounting metaphysical investigations as meaningless.

Frege's work was devoted to demonstrating that arithmetic could be reduced to logic (logicism). This meant rejecting psychologism and empiricism, the two dominant philosophical positions of the time. Psychologism holds that the truths of philosophy are founded upon psychology; empiricism says that the truths of arithmetic exist independent of logic, and are rooted in experience. Again, Kant is the starting point for groundbreaking work. Frege agreed with Kant that knowledge of mathematics is a priori; but he rejected the Kantian view that our knowledge of mathematics is *synthetic* a priori (dependent upon intuition). Frege said that knowledge of mathematics is a priori in an *analytic* sense, and only depends upon logic for its proof. Frege's goal was to discover a purely logical grounding for number theory, but in pursuing it he would also create an analysis of language and its relation to logic and truth.

Frege's *Concept-Script* (1879) is generally held to be the most important advance in logic since Aristotle. In his quest for a mathematical proof from pure logic Frege created a notation system that could express arguments, while avoiding the problems of clarity inherent in colloquial language. He also developed a propositional calculus and a predicate calculus, which allowed for the representation and analysis of increasingly complex sentences. Here Frege not only grounded his logical investigations in arithmetic, but he also developed ideas that would lead to what has been called the 'linguistic turn' in philosophy. Frege's *The Foundations of Arithmetic* (1884) is considered the first work of analytic philosophy, and lays down three rules central to it: first, to avoid psychologism by separating the psychological from the logical, and to distinguish between the subjective and the objective; second, to observe the 'context principle', which says the meaning of a word is never found in isolation, only in the context of a proposition; and third, to respect the distinction between concept and object that defines a number as an object independent of mind.

The next man of importance was Frege, who published his first work in 1879, and his definition of 'number' in 1884; but, in spite of the epoch-making nature of his discoveries, he remained wholly without recognition until I drew attention to him in 1903.

Bertrand Russell, *A History of Western Philosophy* (1945)

Bergson and intuitionism

The French philosopher Henri Bergson (1859–1941) mistrusted empiricism and instead advocated a philosophy based on intuition. Bergson's sense of intuition does not refer to some vague feeling about things; it was as rigorous as any empirical method of investigation. He defined intuition in *Creative Evolution* (1907) as an 'instinct that has become disinterested, self-conscious, capable of reflecting upon its object and of enlarging it indefinitely'. Bergson is also responsible for the concept of *élan vital*. This idea of a 'vital impulse' referred to natural phenomena in evolution that reductive methods could not explain. He also described the phenomenon of *duration* or 'lived time'. This concept refers to the way in which we experience time as a stream, rather than a series of separate moments.

> A truly intuitive philosophy would realize the union so greatly desired, of metaphysics and science.
>
> Henri Bergson, *The Creative Mind: An Introduction to Metaphysics* (1934) (trans. Mabelle L. Andison, 1946)

Like Brentano and Husserl, Bergson began his studies with logic and mathematics, being particularly adept at the former and gaining early renown for solving a mathematical problem that had been identified by Pascal in the seventeenth century. It was this grounding in scientific method that gave weight to Bergson's later elaboration of a theory of intuition. He also highlighted the importance of embodiment as the locus of experience of self and others, space and time – a theme that has become perennial in European philosophy over the past seventy-five years.

Bergson was the greatest popularizer of philosophy in the early twentieth century. In 1913 he lectured at Columbia University, where the crowd that came to see him is said to have created the first traffic jam ever recorded in New York City. Although he was a Jew, Bergson was drawn to the Roman Catholic Church – a fidelity he maintained in spite of the fact that the Church placed three of his books on the *Index Librorum Prohibitorum*. A Roman Catholic priest said prayers at his funeral. Bergson died – luckily for him, perhaps – in 1942, just before the French authorities began deporting Jews to the Nazi death camps.

Freud and the unconscious

The dominance of empiricism was further challenged by the Austrian neurologist Sigmund Freud (1856–1939), who identified the unconscious as a vital component of the human mind, and described the importance of sexuality in our development and behaviour.

Freud constructed a new topography of the mind with three components: *id*, *ego* and *superego*. The id is instinct, driven by the pleasure principle to avoid anxiety. The ego is the rational self, which manages the *reality principle* and translates instincts into socially acceptable behaviour. The superego internalizes external authority and is the site of conscience and morality. With Josef Breuer (1842–1925) Freud developed psychoanalysis, a method for treating neuroses – a form of functional mental illness (as opposed to organic mental disease) – caused by imbalances in the relations between id, ego and superego. The analysis of dreams for some kind of symbolic content was an important part of psychoanalysis for Freud, and *The Interpretation of Dreams* (1900) is one of the defining books of the twentieth century.

Obviously one must hold oneself responsible for the evil impulses of one's dreams. In what other way can one deal with them? Unless the content of the dream rightly understood is inspired by alien spirits, it is part of my own being.

Sigmund Freud, *The Interpretation of Dreams* (additional notes, 1925 edition) (trans. James Strachey)

Psychoanalysis has proven to be much more than a therapeutic method. It is a tool for the analysis of all kinds of social, political and literary phenomena, an additional twentieth-century hermeneutic. Freud himself touched on some of the areas amenable to analysis in *The Psychopathology of Everyday Life* (1901), *Jokes and their Relation to the Unconscious* (1905), *Totem and Taboo* (1913), *Civilization and Its Discontents* (1930), and *Moses and Monotheism* (1939). Freud's contemporaries in psychoanalysis included Carl Jung (1875–1961), whose interest lay in identifying ruling archetypes in psychology; Otto Rank (1884–1939), who explored the significance of legend, myth and art to psychoanalysis; and Wilhelm Reich (1897–1957), a most unusual thinker who believed that the orgasm is the basis of mental health.

Freud is one of three thinkers to emerge from the nineteenth century who changed the way we think, because they changed the way in which we understand the hidden structure of things. Darwin described the action of natural selection as the mechanism behind the origin of species; Karl Marx devised the theoretical tools to explain the hitherto unexplained relations of capital and labour that shape history; and Freud provided a map of the hidden mind, a guide to the unconscious, and supplied the missing motives for much human behaviour that had previously perplexed psychologists.

Durkheim, Weber and the rise of sociology

The French sociologist Émile Durkheim (1858–1917) was quick to take up Auguste Comte's positivism and develop it into a sociological method, which he outlined in *Rules of the Sociological Method* (1895). Now sociology would exist as an academic discipline that owed much to philosophy, but was separate from it. The vindication of Durkheim's method was his 1897 masterpiece *Suicide*, a work that both demonstrates sociological method and continues to be read today as a standard text on the subject.

Durkheim's principal legacy to Western thought is his concept of the *social fact*. In *Rules of the Sociological Method* he defines these as facts outside the control of the individual and which actually *control* him (what social scientists would later call 'social control'). The social fact is important because it reverses the hitherto dominant idealist view in German thought that the individual is the creator of his world. Durkheim took man away from himself and placed him in an external world that would be explored in detail by structuralists such as Ferdinand de Saussure, Claude Lévi-Strauss (1908–2009), Roland Barthes (1915–80), and by the Nietzsche-influenced French philosopher Michel Foucault (1926–84).

Max Weber (1864–1920) followed Comte and Durkheim as a thinker who developed sociology as a powerful academic discipline. He differed markedly from both predecessors in that he rejected positivism and shifted the focus of sociology to the individual; he was interested in what happens to individuals as a result of social action. Weber was first to identify the process of *rationalization* by which modern bureaucracies turned human beings into cogs in a machine. This is how the Nazis were able to turn a functionary like Adolf Eichmann (1906–62) into a man who resigned his conscience and sent millions of Jews to their deaths in the gas chambers – the phenomenon explored by the political philosopher Hannah Arendt in *Eichmann in Jerusalem: A Report on the Banality of Evil* (1963). Through rationalization, people come to accept rules designed for maximum efficiency, but which might be at odds with traditional moral teaching.

Weber's most important work is *The Protestant Ethic and the Spirit of Capitalism* (1905), in which he develops the concept of *elective affinity*. Weber uses this to describe the situation whereby, according to his thesis, the innate affinity of Protestantism and capitalism enabled their joint rise to power. A by-product of this elective affinity is rationalization, leaving man imprisoned in an 'iron cage' of ends-means efficiency. While Weber was critical of capitalism, he was also wary of socialism, which he believed would create an ever-larger bureaucracy, leading to more rationalization and more iron cages.

British idealism comes of age

British universities had always maintained a fondness for Plato and Neoplatonism, partly because the English public school system was thoroughly imbued with a spirit of philhellenism. Idealism, therefore, kept a foothold in the British intellectual establishment despite the powerful empiricism of Locke, Hume and Mill. The Romantic poets Wordsworth and Coleridge and the Victorian poet and critic Matthew Arnold (1822–88) were all proponents of Kant, and they kept the spirit of German idealism alive for the general reading public. In British universities Kant, Schelling, Fichte and, especially, Hegel, all figured prominently on the philosophy syllabus.

During the second half of the nineteenth century, most of the leading philosophers in British universities were followers of Hegel. While it seems odd to say this now, when British philosophy has been analytic for more than a century, in the second half of the nineteenth century Hegelianism *was* British philosophy. So, when historians talk about *British idealism*, all they are referring to is British philosophy in general in the late nineteenth century.

The most important British idealist was F. H. Bradley (1846–1924), whose *Appearance and Reality* (1893) was the subject of the American-English poet T. S. Eliot's (1888–1965) doctoral dissertation at Harvard, *Knowledge and Experience in the Philosophy of*

F. H. Bradley (1964). Other important idealists include T. H. Green (1836–82), Bernard Bosanquet (1848–1923), J. M. E. McTaggart (1866–1925), H. H. Joachim (1868–1938), J. H. Muirhead (1855–1940) and G. R. G. Mure (1893–1979).

The very soul of the Absolute which I defend is its insistence and emphasis on an all-pervasive relativism. Everything is justified as being real in its own sphere and degree, but not so as to entitle it to invade other spheres, and, whether positively or negatively, to usurp other powers.

F. H. Bradley, *Essays on Truth and Reality* (1914)

Bradley was an extreme monist. He conceived the world as a unity and, following Hegel, he called it the Absolute (unlike Descartes, who was a mind-body dualist). The focus of Bradley's inquiry was the relationship between thought and reality. Bradley didn't just reject the empiricism of Bentham and Mill, he also rejected their liberal political philosophy – but on logical grounds. In *Ethical Studies* (1876) Bradley said utilitarianism gives community precedence over the individual; in contrast, he argued, the good is achieved by the individual's contribution to community and the common good. Bradley's *The Principles of Logic* (1922) argues for wholeness and unity as opposed to an atomistic worldview.

Bradley was strongly influenced by T. H. Green, the Oxford

idealist who started the movement against empiricism and utilitarianism. He was a Kantian who held that everything in the world is constituted by human consciousness. He disagreed with Kant in arguing that the noumenal world (or things-in-themselves) can be known, because a single, eternal Mind unifies everything. Bernard Bosanquet was a colleague of Bradley's who took seriously Green's call for 'active citizenship', and resigned his fellowship at University College, Oxford, to do social work and teach adult education classes.

Unlike Bradley and his colleagues, J. M. E. McTaggart was at Cambridge rather than Oxford, and he taught both Bertrand Russell and his fellow analytic G. E. Moore (1873–1958). It was from McTaggart that Russell caught his early and short-lived enthusiasm for Hegel, which would eventually give way to a conversion of Damascene proportions when he abandoned idealism for logicism. McTaggart was an important interpreter of Hegel and his works include *The Unreality of Time* (1908) and *The Nature of Existence* (1921, 1927).

Husserl and phenomenology

In many ways the German philosopher Edmund Husserl (1859–1938) represents the end of Kantian idealism. Though now remembered as the father of phenomenology, Husserl first studied mathematics with Leo Königsberger (1837–1921) and Carl Weierstrass (1815–97), and took a PhD in the subject. Thereafter he studied with Franz Brentano, who introduced him to Aquinas's concept of intentionality. Husserl used this to describe the relationship between consciousness and its objects (the formulation of consciousness as *consciousness is always consciousness of something*).

First, anyone who seriously intends to become a philosopher must 'once in his life' withdraw into himself and attempt, within himself, to overthrow and build anew all the sciences that, up to then, he has been accepting. Philosophy – wisdom (*sagesse*) – is the philosopher's quite personal affair. It must arise as his wisdom, as his self-acquired knowledge tending toward universality, a knowledge for which he can answer from the beginning, and at each step, by virtue of his own absolute insights.

Edmund Husserl, *Cartesian Meditations* (1931)

(trans. Dorion Cairns, 1950)

Husserl's early phenomenology, presented in *Logical Investigations* (1900, 1901), focused on objects rather than subjects and was the source of a new philosophical rallying cry: *to the things themselves!* It was a major move away from Kantian idealism. In his last work, *The Crisis of the European Sciences* (1936), Husserl was careful to distance his phenomenology from Kantian idealism (he always referred to phenomenology as a science). He thought that Kant promoted 'a metaphysics in the dangerous sense inimical to all genuine science'. In the *Crisis* he also criticized narrowly empirical and analytical thought. He believed that phenomenology would be the source of 'a total transformation of the task of knowledge'.

Phenomenology was the dominant trend in twentieth-century continental philosophy, and its influence continues in that tradition today. For this reason, Husserl is the most influential philosopher since Kant. Without Husserl there would be no Heidegger, Maurice Merleau-Ponty or a hundred other thinkers, including Lacan, Derrida, Hans-Georg Gadamer (1900–2002) and Julia Kristeva (*b*.1941). There would be no existentialism, no hermeneutics, no post-structuralism.

The analytic–continental divide

In 1894 Gottlob Frege published a highly critical review of Husserl's *Philosophy of Arithmetic* (1891) in *Zeitschrift für Philosophie und philosophische Kritik* (103, 1894). It was a defining moment in the history of Western thought, when two philosophers, heirs of a common European tradition, drew a line in the sand over arithmetic. For his part, Husserl used descriptive psychology and logic in his attempt to create a theory of number. Frege's method was to try to derive principles of mathematics purely from logic. In his review, Frege accused Husserl of psychologism – the tendency to derive facts or laws of (in this case) mathematics from those found in psychology (though both Locke and Hume had also been 'guilty' of psychologism). Frege further accused Husserl of creating abstractions that would 'cleanse things of their peculiarities . . . in the wash-tub of the mind'.

> Of all philosophers, perhaps of all theorists of any kind, Frege pursued, in his work, the most extraordinary single-minded course.
>
> Michael Dummett, *The Interpretation of Frege's Philosophy* (1987)

Frege's pursuit of an analytic a priori grounding of arithmetic in logic was leading to a methodology that would try to reduce all philosophical problems to a few that were amenable to solution by logicism. Husserl's goal was to start with arithmetic and logic and move towards an investigation of the entire lifeworld (*Lebenswelt*). Frege's cause was taken up by Bertrand Russell, the greatest English philosopher of the twentieth century.

Russell took a first in mathematics at Trinity College, Cambridge, in 1893 where, under the influence of J. M. E. McTaggart and F. H. Bradley, he was briefly a Hegelian idealist; but Russell lost his admiration for metaphysics after meeting G. E. Moore. Russell's important early works were *The Principles of Mathematics* (1903) and *Principia Mathematica* (1910–13). By 1901 he became convinced that Frege's logicism would become the foundation of the new analytical philosophy. A key founding work of this doctrine was Russell's essay 'On Denoting' (1905), which challenged the view of his godfather John Stuart Mill that mathematics could be reduced to generalizations from previous experience. For his part, G. E. Moore also abandoned his previous attempts to ground an ethics in post-Kantian idealism with his 1903 paper 'The Refutation of Idealism'. It sounded the death knell for idealism in Britain, and it did for ethics what Russell did for logic. Moore's *Principia Ethica* (1903) remains his most significant work, and is a landmark statement of a naturalist theory of ethics in the modern period.

Modern Idealism, if it asserts any general conclusion about the universe at all, asserts that it is spiritual. There are two points about this assertion to which I wish to call attention. These points are that, whatever be its exact meaning, it is certainly meant to assert (1) that the universe is very different indeed from what it seems, and (2) that it has quite a large number of properties which it does not seem to have.

G. E. Moore, 'The Refutation of Idealism' (1903)

In addition to bringing Frege to the attention of the philosophical establishment, Russell was instrumental in persuading the Viennese-born Ludwig Wittgenstein (1889–1951) to pursue a career in philosophy rather than aircraft engineering. The young Wittgenstein was attracted to the logicism of Russell and Frege, and his *Tractatus Logico-Philosophicus* (1921) argued that language can be reduced to 'atoms' of meaning relating to states of affairs or facts. Russell arranged for the publication of the *Tractatus* and also contributed an introduction to the book, which guaranteed it would be noticed by the widest possible audience. In his introduction Russell wrote: 'The essential business of language is to assert or deny facts.' Thus Russell declared that philosophy was in fact the philosophy of language.

3.001 'A state of affairs is thinkable': what this means is that we can picture it to ourselves.

3.01 The totality of true thoughts is a picture of the world.

3.02 A thought contains the possibility of the situation of which it is the thought. What is thinkable is possible too.

Ludwig Wittgenstein, *Tractatus Logico-Philosophicus* (1921)

(trans. D. F. Pears and B. F. McGuinness, 1961)

Wittgenstein is important to the Anglo-American tradition of analytic philosophy in the way that Husserl is for the continental tradition. Just as the early Husserl had much in common with Frege and other mathematicians of the era, so aspects of Wittgenstein's work can be seen to belong in the tradition of Kierkegaard, Schopenhauer and Nietzsche. From the latter, Wittgenstein borrowed a beguiling aphoristic style unlike any other in modern philosophy. Additionally, he was concerned throughout his life with human rather than purely logical problems, and these concerns eventually show in his later work as he revised his position on language.

In the *Tractatus* Wittgenstein develops a picture theory of meaning. He compares language to musical notation, which he then, in turn, likens to the pictorial form of the state of affairs of a musical composition. While Russell and Moore were bent on destroying metaphysics, Wittgenstein ended the *Tractatus* on a more modest and respectful note: 'What we cannot speak about we must pass over in silence.' After the First World War Wittgenstein gave up the logical atomism of the *Tractatus* with its assumption that the meaning of a word is the thing that it stands for. Instead he devised the idea of 'language games', as a result of reflecting on how children acquire and use language.

I once asked G. E. Moore what he thought of Wittgenstein. 'I think very well of him,' he said. I asked why, and he replied: 'Because at my lectures he looks puzzled, and nobody else ever looks puzzled.'

Bertrand Russell, *Autobiography* (1967)

Wittgenstein died in 1951, but important works by him continued to be published. A central text is his *Philosophical Investigations* (1953), a founding document of what was called the ordinary language school of philosophy at Oxford, whose proponents included Gilbert Ryle (1900–76) and J. L. Austin (1911–60). Wittgenstein was wracked with existential doubt and angst all of his life. The son of Jewish parents who converted to Lutheranism, he struggled with belief in God, especially during his time at the front in the First World War. He eventually moved towards Roman Catholicism, and was given a Catholic burial. His last writings were an attempt to refute doubt and scepticism, and resulted in the book *On Certainty* (1969).

The birth of post-imperialist philosophy

During the American and French revolutions, philosophers applied Enlightenment ideas to politics, resulting in real political change as well as a new set of abstract political principles emphasizing the equality of man. But this equality did not generally apply to people of colour. The Indian barrister Mohandas K. Gandhi (1869–1948) drew on the American transcendentalist Henry David Thoreau's ideas of civil disobedience to develop the theory and practice of nonviolent protest against government repression and institutionalized racism.

Gandhi drew upon Hinduism, Jainism, Islam and Christianity. The central idea of his non-violent philosophy derives from the doctrine of *ahimsa* (common to Jainism, Hinduism and Buddhism), which prohibits injuring or killing living beings. Simply stated, Gandhi's theory of nonviolence is: *God is truth. The way to truth lies through* ahimsa.

Gandhi's theory of non-violence was first applied in British-ruled South Africa, where he stood up for the civil rights of Indians. Returning to his native India, Gandhi spent his life pursing various non-violent campaigns. His philosophy culminates in the concept of *satyagraha*, which means 'holding fast to the truth'. Gandhi taught the tautology 'God is truth' but 'truth is God'. God did not need to be a person or a thing. Gandhi's ideas are laid out in *An Autobiography, or the Story of My Experiments with Truth* (1927).

A nation that wants to come into its own ought to know all the ways and means to freedom. Usually they include violence as the last remedy. *Satyagraha*, on the other hand, is an absolutely non-violent weapon. I regard it as my duty to explain its practice and its limitations.

Mohandas K. Gandhi, *An Autobiography,*
or the Story of My Experiments with Truth (1927)

In the United States, the African-American sociologist and civil-rights activist W. E. B. Du Bois (1868–1963) took a double-edged sword to the institutionalized racism of his country by using its institutions to educate himself, and then by creating new institutions to combat racism. He began by going to Harvard, where he absorbed the ideas of William James and George Santayana. He studied Hegel and Marx, and developed a thesis that capitalism is based on slavery. He spent two years studying in Berlin, and in his autobiographical book *Darkwater* (1920) he describes the pleasure he felt in Europe, where he was not judged by the colour of his skin. And then, he wrote, 'I dropped suddenly back into "nigger"-hating America!'

Is it possible, and probable, that nine millions of men can make effective progress in economic lines if they are deprived of political rights, made a servile caste, and allowed only the most meagre chance for developing their exceptional men? If history and reason give any distinct answer to these questions, it is an emphatic *No*.

W. E. B. Du Bois, *The Souls of Black Folk* (1903)

Du Bois was the first African-American to take a PhD at Harvard. In his thesis on 'The Suppression of the African Slave-Trade to the United States 1638–1870' (1896) he attacked the views of the African-American educator and orator Booker T. Washington (1856–1915) for not being sufficiently critical of the treatment of blacks in the United States. Du Bois was the first to focus on the economic causes of crime, poverty and social malaise in *The Philadelphia Negro* (1899). He co-founded the National Association for the Advancement of Colored People (NAACP), but moved increasingly to the Left, leaving the NAACP in 1948. He joined the Communist Party aged ninety-three and emigrated to Ghana in 1961, where he died. Du Bois set the agenda for the American civil rights movement, whose leaders would include Martin Luther King, but also for the Black Panthers. He was a supporter of Pan-Africanism, an idea taken forward by the Trinidadian historian C. L. R. James (1901–89), whose *World Revolution* (1937) criticized colonialism from a Marxist perspective.

The First World War and philosophy

The First World War (1914–18), which claimed the lives of seventeen million people (some seven million of them civilians) was a cataclysmic event in modern history that left no aspect of life untouched – including philosophy.

After the Renaissance, philosophy had tended to be a supranational unifying force, a kind of international language in which arguments were won and lost, but usually at the cost only of inferior ideas, rather than blood (philosophy regarded as a kind of bloodless battle of ideas). Though often national in character – as is evident from the English, Scottish, German and French Enlightenments – philosophy's natural tendency was international, even universal, where the truth was concerned.

This changed with the outbreak of the First World War, and some idea of how this disastrous failure of nations to avoid carnage affected philosophy and philosophers can be obtained by looking at the fortunes of the founding fathers of analytic philosophy, Wittgenstein, Russell and Moore. The declaration of war naturally interrupted their friendship. For instance, Wittgenstein felt obliged to return to Austria, where he joined the army and served throughout the conflict, composing early drafts of the *Tractatus* while struggling with thoughts of suicide and with doubts about Christian belief.

After the war, intellectual cooperation among philosophers and scientists in Britain, France and Germany gradually resumed. The Vienna Circle, a group of philosophers and mathematicians who developed *logical positivism*, formed around Moritz Schlick (1882–1936), Rudolf Carnap (1891–1970), and Kurt Gödel (1906–78). They were joined by the British philosopher A. J. Ayer (1910–89) and the American W. V. Quine (1908–2000). Logical positivism is the doctrine that all knowledge is strictly empirical or experiential and that the method for understanding empirical knowledge is *symbolic logic*. In the other tradition, Husserl attracted a number of students from the United States, including Marvin Farber (1901–80), Dorion Cairns (1901–73), William Ernest Hocking (1873–1966) and Fritz Kaufmann (1891–1958).

The age of uncertainty

After the First World War, uncertainty took hold. The numerous challenges to empiricism – from thinkers as diverse as Bergson and Husserl – seemed to exacerbate analytic philosophy's desire to reduce problems to manageable proportions, so they could be identified and solved definitively. The opposing tendency – continental philosophy – tended to embrace uncertainty, even recognizing it as being at the heart of the kinds of existential questions they chose to tackle. To this highly charged atmosphere we must add Albert Einstein's (1879–1955) discovery of the Special Theory of Relativity in 1903.

Einstein upset Newton's applecart by developing the theory that space and time are not separate phenomena, but part of a unified whole called *spacetime*. The concept of spacetime, developed by Hermann Minkowski (1864–1909), described a world with four dimensions – the three dimensions of space (length, width, depth), plus the added dimension of time. This made scientific knowledge a more complicated affair. Now scientists realized that when they observed an object what they saw depended upon their position relative to it in space and time. In 1905 Einstein published a paper describing the photoelectric effect in which light has the dual nature of being both a wave and a particle, depending upon how it is observed. For 1,500 years philosophy and science had striven for certainty. Now, at the point where the most advanced science and philosophy collided, it became apparent that any claim to absolute knowledge is questionable, and that knowledge is dependent upon the perspective of the observer. As Bergson had pointed out, the investigator makes observations from his position as embodied – from a certain place, time and point of view – which is to say, from a limited perspective. But when there are many observers there are many observations, a multiplicity of points of view, so the search for knowledge based upon objectivity is thrown into question.

> The most beautiful experience we can have is the mysterious. It is the fundamental emotion that stands at the cradle of true art and true science. Whoever does not know it and can no longer wonder, no longer marvel, is as good as dead, and his eyes are dimmed.
>
> Albert Einstein, 'The World as I See It' (1934)

Along with a revolution in science, the early twentieth century saw the application of Marxist theory in the October Revolution of 1917. This led to the Russian Civil War (1917–22) and the formation of the first socialist state, the Soviet Union (or Union of Soviet Socialist Republics). Until now the work of Marx and Engels had offered theoretical analyses of the relationship between capital and labour, as well as historical predictions about the demise of capitalism. However, Vladimir Ilyich Lenin (1870–1924) used Marxist theory to analyse capitalism in relation to its late imperialist phase, and in *State and Revolution* (1917) he outlined a programme for a dictatorship of the proletariat. The Leninist version of Marxism became the official version of state socialism in the Soviet Union, which would survive until 1991. Lenin's defence of Marx in *State and Revolution* is typical of how Marxism evolved in the twentieth century, with successive interpreters claiming to understand the 'real' or 'true' Marx.

> . . . 'the special repressive force' for the suppression of the proletariat by the bourgeoisie, of millions of labouring people by a handful or two of the wealthy, must be replaced by a 'special repressive force' for the suppression of the bourgeoisie by the proletariat (the dictatorship of the proletariat). This is the very nub of 'the eradication of the state as a state'.
>
> Vladimir Ilyich Lenin, *State and Revolution* (1917)
>
> (trans. Robert Service, 1992)

Lenin's socialism was intended to make man free, but in reality the Soviet system became a corrupt and bloated totalitarian bureaucracy, ruled by card-carrying members of the Communist Party. Ordinary citizens (who weren't members of the Party) had their freedoms curtailed. Under the Soviet dictator Josef Stalin (1878–1953) ideological purges and the killing of perceived political enemies became commonplace. In the Great Purge (1936–38), Stalin's secret police, the NKVD, killed up to 1.2 million citizens regarded as dangerous to the regime. The Great Purge has been compared to the Reign of Terror (1793–4) that followed the French Revolution, in which an estimated 40,000 people died.

The Russian Revolution (1917) was of supreme importance for Western philosophy, because it asked the question of all thinking people: are you for or against it? Before the Revolution, Marx was just another philosopher to be mentioned in the same breath as Hegel. After the Revolution Marxist thought was no longer regarded merely as a tool for 'doing' philosophy, economics or history. It became a creed, a state religion, an alternative not only to capitalism but to Christianity. It would be many years before the truth of Stalin's purges, and the elaborate system of gulags (forced labour camps in remote regions of the Soviet Union) would come to light. Many left-leaning European and American philosophers supported the Soviet Union (or used their support of the Soviet Union to signal their dissatisfaction with capitalism and imperialism). In the same way that Christianity splintered into countless sects, so Marxists multiplied, defining themselves on the basis of doctrinal and theoretical differences.

The most famous Marxist theoretical group was the Frankfurt School, whose leading lights included the German philosophers Max Horkheimer (1895–1973), Theodor Adorno (1903–69) and Erich Fromm (1900–80). Disaffected both with capitalism and communism, the Frankfurt School combined Marxist criticism with sociology, existentialism, hermeneutics and psychoanalysis to address a broad range of social, political and aesthetic issues. One of the most important Marxist thinkers of the period was the Italian Antonio Gramsci (1891–1937), who identified the concept of *cultural hegemony* as the means by which the capitalist state maintained its ideological grip. He died after a long period of imprisonment under the regime of the Fascist dictator Benito Mussolini (1883–1945), and his *Prison Notebooks* (1929–33) are required reading for students of Marxism.

Heidegger, Jaspers and *Existenzphilosophie*

After the First World War Martin Heidegger (1889–1976) was on his way to becoming the most important philosopher in Germany. Heidegger was Husserl's assistant, his most distinguished pupil, and Husserl regarded him as his intellectual heir. But Heidegger was impatient with Husserl's approach to philosophy as a constant search for beginnings and the careful application of method. Heidegger was eager to reach a destination, and in turning away from his master he became one of three creators of *Existenz-philosophie* or early existentialism, along with his German colleague Karl Jaspers (1883–1969) and their Danish predecessor Sören Kierkegaard. Heidegger's philosophy is built upon the characterization of *Dasein* ('being-there' or 'existence') as temporal in nature. His early work *Being and Time* (1927) is his most enduring.

By casting light on the source of the 'time' 'in which' entities within-the-world are encountered – time as 'within-timeness' – we shall make manifest an essential possibility of the temporalizing of temporality.

Martin Heidegger, *Being and Time* (1927)

(trans. John Macquarrie and Edward Robinson, 1962)

Heidegger sought to break from the neo-Kantianism of the time by returning to the classical philosophy of ancient Greece for his starting point. He has been compared to the Greek philosopher Heraclitus, who famously said that it is impossible to step twice into the same river. For Heidegger, this was an essential aspect of *Dasein*, which was further characterized as a *being-towards-death*.

Heidegger believed that the German language was the great modern language of philosophy (and poetry), rather as the Greek language had been in the classical era. This conviction took on an unpleasant nationalist dimension, building on the views of Fichte and other German idealists. Defeat in the First World War and the humiliation of the Treaty of Versailles (1919) bred an atmosphere of resentment in Germany. As time went on, the German people began to feel they had been punished enough for their role in the war. For Heidegger, Germany seemed squeezed between the twin evils of the communism of the Soviet Union and the gross consumerism of the United States. These preconditions, along with his penchant for a philosophy rooted in German blood and soil, made him susceptible to the appeal of Adolf Hitler (1889–1945). Heidegger joined the Nazi Party and was made rector of the University of Freiburg in 1933, where he gave a notorious introductory address that concluded with three shouts of 'Heil Hitler!'

I saw in the movement that had gained power [the Nazi Party] the possibility of an inner recollection and renewal of the people and a path that would allow it to discover its historical vocation in the Western world.

Martin Heidegger, 'The Self-Assertion of the German University' (1933) (trans. Karsten Harries, 1985)

Karl Jaspers is the unsung hero of mid-twentieth century philosophy, a Mahler to Heidegger's Wagner. His existentialist philosophy was based – like that of Husserl's German-Jewish student Edith Stein (1891–1942) and the German theologian Dietrich Bonhoeffer (1906–45) – on the possibility of intersubjectivity, rooted in love and empathy. Subjects who fully recognized the subjectivity of the other would promote dialogue and avoid conflict.

> When man reaches for his highest possibilities, he may deceive himself most radically. He may fall down all the steps he has climbed and end up lower than he was at the beginning. To preserve his being he must hold fast to every mode of reasonableness, for this alone preserves for him the meaning of his intellectual acquisitions.
>
> Karl Jaspers, *Philosophy of Existence* (1938)
> (trans. Richard F. Grabau, 1971)

Jaspers's education was perhaps the deepest and the widest of any of his contemporaries. After reading law, he took PhDs in medicine and psychology, before eventually becoming professor of philosophy at Heidelberg. Influenced by Kant, Husserl, Nietzsche and Kierkegaard, Jaspers questioned prevailing methods of psychiatric diagnosis; he began to inquire beyond diagnostic labels and to study the biographies of patients in an effort to discover the individual nature of their illnesses. His biographical method, then revolutionary, is now an everyday part of psychiatric practice. His two-volume work *General Psychopathology* (1913) became a standard text.

Jaspers incorporated the hermeneutics of Dilthey and Schelling in his *Psychology of Worldviews* (1919). While Jaspers started out as a scientist, and was much influenced by Kierkegaard, he mistrusted the sense of absolute objectivity in science. A deeply spiritual man, he did not, however, believe in a personal God. He cultivated an interest in the social sciences, numbering among his friends and colleagues the German sociologists Max Weber (1864–1920) and Georg Simmel (1858–1918), and the Hungarian Marxist and literary theorist Georg Lukács (1885–1971). Jaspers was trying to derive a method from Kant's transcendental idealism via the emerging social sciences and his own experience as a psychiatrist to describe the inner life of the subject (and to continue Kant's project of investigating human freedom). He began to incorporate the phenomenological attitude in treating psychiatric patients, and in so doing identified the *limit-situation* as a moment when the subject faces extreme guilt or anxiety, the embracing of which opened up the possibility for transcendence. Jaspers was ultimately concerned with intersubjectivity, with the possibilities for communication with each other and our own individual transcendence through a process he described as *loving struggle*.

National Socialism and philosophy

Fascist ideology never had a catechism like Marxism had in *The Communist Manifesto*. It did, however, find some foundation in the work of the British-born writer Houston Stewart Chamberlain (1855–1927), whose *The Foundations of the Nineteenth Century* (1899) outlined pan-Germanic ideals and fanned the flames of an increasingly overt anti-Semitism in Germany. The founding text of the National Socialist Party in Germany is Adolf Hitler's *Mein Kampf* (*My Struggle*, 1925–6). Hitler believed that communism and the Jews were responsible for Germany's perilous economic situation after the First World War, and that a struggle against them would restore the greatness of the nation.

After Hitler came to power in Germany in 1933, the leading Nazi Party philosophers were Alfred Baeumler (1887–1968) and Alfred Rosenberg (1893–1946). Baeumler was responsible for misreading Friedrich Nietzsche's philosophy so as to co-opt the popular (and conveniently dead) author to the Nazi cause. This work was carried out with the enthusiastic support of Nietzsche's sister, Elisabeth Förster-Nietzsche (1846–1935). Nietzsche himself detested anti-Semitism, and referred to himself as 'an anti-anti-Semite'. Rosenberg's task was to organize various aspects of National Socialist belief into some kind of coherent philosophy. He was later found guilty of crimes against humanity at the post-war Nuremberg Trials (1945–6) and hanged, along with other leading Nazis.

University professors in Nazi Germany faced a moral choice: join the National Socialist Party and enjoy preferment, or refuse and be sidelined. More than 50 per cent of philosophy professors in Germany joined the Party. Karl Jaspers did not. He steadfastly resisted the Nazis and protected his Jewish wife, with whom he survived the war. Edith Stein, Husserl's assistant before Heidegger, converted to Catholicism and became a nun, using her position to petition Pope Pius XII to intervene to protect Germany's Jews (although he did nothing). Stein was taken by the Gestapo from a convent in Holland and sent to Auschwitz, where she was killed. The Lutheran theologian Dietrich Bonhoeffer was a double agent for the German resistance inside German military intelligence, and was part of a plot to kill Hitler. He was hanged at Flossenbürg concentration camp. Jaspers, Stein and Bonhoeffer were thinkers with the moral courage to live by their beliefs.

Exodus of philosophers from Germany

At the start of the Second World War Ludwig Wittgenstein was living and working in England. The son of an Austrian Jew who had converted to Lutheranism, Wittgenstein would have been at risk had he returned home to Nazi-occupied Austria. The British economist John Maynard Keynes (1883–1946) intervened on Wittgenstein's behalf and arranged for his naturalization as a British citizen to be fast-tracked.

Leading members of the Vienna Circle of logical positivists left Germany while they could. Foremost among them was Rudolf Carnap (1891–1970), who helped to make the University of Chicago a centre for logical positivism. Carnap is especially interesting because he studied under Husserl for two years before going on to become a student of Frege's – so he was exposed to the teaching of the respective fathers of the continental and analytic traditions. Carnap's philosophy was profoundly informed by Russell's *Principia Mathematica*. His most influential work was *The Logical Syntax of Language* (1934), which in turn had a great impact on the English philosopher A. J. Ayer. In his *Language, Truth and Logic* (1936), one of the best-selling books in the history of English-language philosophy, Ayer developed the *verification principle*, which holds that statements containing propositions that cannot be verified – for instance, all of those in metaphysics and theology – are, literally, meaningless. For those of the analytic persuasion, Ayer had, at a stroke, finished the job that Frege and Russell had started with the demolition of idealism in Britain. Indeed, Ayer said on several occasions that, after him, the work of philosophy was done.

> Metaphysicians are musicians without musical ability.
>
> Rudolf Carnap, 'The Elimination of Metaphysics through
>
> Logical Analysis of Language' (1932)
>
> (trans. Arthur Pap, 1959)

Karl Popper (1902–94), the leading philosopher of science in the modern period, also fled the Nazis. An Austrian Jew, Popper first went to New Zealand, before settling in Britain. Popper made two major contributions to Western philosophy. The first was to develop the philosophy of science as a discipline in its own right. In *The Logic of Scientific Discovery* (1935) and *Conjectures and Refutations* (1963), Popper described how scientific theories are formed, why some survive, and why others don't. He rejected the verification principle of the logical positivists and argued precisely the opposite – that *falsifiability* is the proper criterion for truth. Popper called his approach *critical rationalism*, and saw himself as continuing work that had been started by Hume and Kant.

Popper's second major contribution to philosophy was his defence of liberal values by identifying historicism (the theory that social and cultural phenomena are determined by history) as the enemy of freedom. His *The Poverty of Historicism* (1957), a series of lectures given in 1936, highlighted the evil that resulted from 'fascist and communist belief in Inexorable Laws of Historical Destiny'. In *The Open Society and Its Enemies* (1945) Popper identified Plato, Hegel and Marx as promoting the historicist creed responsible for the deaths of tens of millions of people.

Hannah Arendt (1906–75) created the discipline of modern political philosophy. In *The Origins of Totalitarianism* (1951) she first outlined the contours of that tendency in detail, tracing its roots in the rise of anti-Semitism in Europe. Arendt studied with Husserl and the German theologian Rudolf Karl Bultmann (1884–1976), but her deepest influence was Heidegger, whose lover she was while an undergraduate at Marburg. Like Heidegger, Arendt had a deep appreciation of ancient Greek philosophy. Unlike Heidegger, who saw man's existence in terms of a *being-towards-death*, Arendt identified the defining human characteristic as *natality*, by which she meant the essential freedom and plenitude of choice that she saw as our true state of being.

The struggle for total domination of the total population of the earth, the elimination of every competing nontotalitarian reality, is inherent in the totalitarian regimes themselves; if they do not pursue global rule as their ultimate goal, they are only too likely to lose whatever power they have already seized.

Hannah Arendt, *The Origins of Totalitarianism* (1951)

In *The Human Condition* (1958) Arendt contrasted two ideas from Greek philosophy, the *via contemplativa* (thinking) and the *via activa* (acting), arguing that it is through action that man achieves freedom. In *Eichmann in Jerusalem: A Report on the Banality of Evil* (1963) Arendt reported on the trial of the Nazi official Adolf Eichmann, whose responsibility it had been to organize the transportation of Jews and other 'enemies of the state' to extermination camps. Unlike the majority of Israelis and diaspora Jews, Arendt disagreed with the characterization of Eichmann as innately evil. In coining the term 'the banality of evil' she argued that Eichmann began life as a clerk who simply followed orders and, through the repetition and alienation of being a small cog in a vast Nazi machine, lost his conscience – a process she estimated took about four weeks. Arendt was concerned, she said, with facts and the truth; her critics, she said, were more interested in maintaining a narrative of 'the Jew as perpetual victim'. The resulting firestorm over this work has raged into the twenty-first century.

Arendt's last work, *The Life of the Mind* (1978) focused on the three stages on the way to man's intellectual maturity: thinking, willing and judging. She died before she could complete the third volume, but the posthumously published *Responsibility and Judgment* (2003) brings together articles and essays that trace her thought on the subject.

The rise and fall of existentialism

German philosophy lost its pre-eminence in the aftermath of the Second World War. German professors who had joined the Nazi Party found themselves in disgrace and out of a job. The Vienna Circle and other analytic philosophers had fled Germany, mostly to the United States. Into this European philosophical vacuum stepped France, which enjoyed an intellectual renaissance from 1945 onwards that rivals its influence in the days of Voltaire and Diderot.

But the shadow of Heidegger fell across it. From 1933 to 1934 the French philosopher Jean-Paul Sartre (1905–80) had visited Nazi Germany to study Husserl's phenomenology and Heidegger's *Existenzphilosophie*. He came back to France and developed Heidegger's work into an existentialist philosophy based on the premise that 'existence precedes essence'. He viewed man as a 'useless passion', whose task is to create meaning through his actions in his lifetime, since there was no afterlife.

Like the great philosophers of the French Enlightenment, Sartre was a literary man as well as a philosopher, and his ideas are often better expressed in his novels than in his sometimes turgid philosophical writings. His novel *Nausea* (1939) opens a window on the existentialist view of the world as its main character is rendered nauseous by the stark 'thing-ness' of objects and absence of meaning in the world. However, Sartre's major statement of existentialist philosophy was *Being and Nothingness* (1945).

> I am sad. One might think that surely I am the sadness in the mode of being what I am. What is the sadness, however, if not the intentional unity which comes to reassemble and animate the totality of my conduct? It is the meaning of this dull look with which I view the world, of my bowed shoulders, of my lowered head, of the listlessness in my whole body.
>
> Jean-Paul Sartre, *Being and Nothingness* (1945)
> (trans. Hazel Barnes, 1956)

For Sartre, man is condemned to be free – a situation termed 'absurd' by the French-Algerian philosopher and novelist Albert Camus (1913–60). In *The Myth of Sisyphus* (1942) Camus borrowed the Greek myth of King Sisyphus, who was condemned to forever roll a great boulder up a hill only for it to roll back down again – a purposeless task without end. Camus compares Sisyphus to the existentialist man, who, by embracing a pointless task, identifies himself.

Inseparable from Sartre was his companion and fellow novelist, diarist and philosopher Simone de Beauvoir (1908–86). She shared many of Sartre's views – indeed, she helped him to formulate them

– but she would make her name internationally with *The Second Sex* (1949), a book that sparked second-wave feminism, a radical break with the first-wave feminism of earlier writers such as Mary Wollstonecraft (1759–97), author of *A Vindication of the Rights of Woman* (1792). Beauvoir's study combined the existentialism she helped to define with Sartre with Marxist analysis and an historical and anthropological survey to present the most detailed account of the position of women to date. Her agenda was extremely radical: she not only advocated intellectual and economic freedom for women, but argued for abortion as a woman's right, and against motherhood, viewing it as incompatible with a life of one's own.

The superiority of the male is, indeed, overwhelming: Perseus, Hercules, David, Achilles, Lancelot, the old French warriors Du Guesclin and Bayard, Napoleon – so many men for one Joan of Arc; and behind her one descries the great male figure of the archangel Michael! Nothing could be more tiresome than the biographies of famous women: they are but pallid figures compared with great men; and most of them bask in the glory of some masculine hero. Eve was not created for her own sake but as a companion for Adam; and she was made from his rib.

Simone de Beauvoir, *The Second Sex* (1949)

(trans. H. M. Parshley, 1953)

Where Sartre had fallen under the spell of Heidegger, his friend Maurice Merleau-Ponty (1908–61) was more attracted to the phenomenology of Husserl. In 1945 he published *Phenomenology of Perception* (1945), in which he takes Husserl's ideas about how the subject constitutes the world around him and combines it with Bergson's ideas about embodiment; Merleau-Ponty also further develops the notion of time as subjectively constituted. *Phenomenology of Perception* is a highly original work, perhaps the most thoroughly executed example of applied phenomenology, and is one of the most enduring works of French existentialism.

> Whether it is a question of another's body or my own, I have no means of knowing the human body other than of living it, which means taking up on my own account the drama which is being played out in it, and losing myself in it. I am my body, at least wholly to the extent that I possess experience, and yet at the same time my body is as it were a 'natural' subject, a provisional sketch of my total being.
>
> Maurice-Merleau Ponty, *Phenomenology of Perception* (1949) (trans. Colin Smith, 1962)

In 1945 Sartre and Beauvoir teamed up with Merleau-Ponty to start a philosophical review, *Les Temps modernes* (*Modern Times*).

All three shared Marxist views, but in 1947 Merleau-Ponty published *Humanism and Terror*, in which he concluded that Stalin's purges were not justified; he and Sartre quarrelled, and in 1948 Merleau-Ponty resigned from *Les Temps modernes*.

Sartre worked for much his life on a long, unfinished defence of Marxism, *Critique of Dialectical Reason* (1960–85). He continued to support the Soviet Union until its violent suppression of the Prague Spring (1968), a brief period of political reform in Czechoslovakia. Thereafter, he lent his support to French groups that followed the thought of Mao Zedong (1893–1976), the Chinese communist leader. Mao's version of Marxism is presented in *Quotations from Chairman Mao Tse-Tung* (1964–76), a collection known in the West as *The Little Red Book*.

Marxism was the prevailing tenor of French thought during its existential period. The most prominent of the French Marxists was the French-Algerian Louis Althusser (1918–90). Althusser's critical importance in post-war philosophy – notably his robust defence of classical Marxism against the reforming tendencies of the many neo-Marxist groups that arose at that time – has been overshadowed by the fact that he strangled his wife while in the grip of an episode of mental illness.

During this period there flourished a strong school of Christian existentialism that did not get noticed as much as the Sartrean variety – Sartre being a brilliant self-publicist, and

France being in need of a great popular philosopher to help rebuild its morale, as well as its public image abroad after the shame of defeat and collaboration in the Second World War. The leading Christian existentialist was Gabriel Marcel (1889–1973), who in fact was the first to use the term 'existentialism', though he later rejected it in favour of 'philosophy of existence' to separate himself from the anti-Christian thought of Sartre and his colleagues.

Marcel was influenced by the German-Jewish philosopher Martin Buber (1878–1965), who argued in his most popular work, *I and Thou* (1923), that God manifests Himself in the context of truly communicative moments between two subjects who recognize in the other the same subjectivity as in themselves. A key concept for Marcel is 'the ontological mystery', which poses human or existential problems that are extra-scientific, and require for their description and understanding a non-reductive methodology. Marcel's best-known works are *Being and Having* (1949) and *The Mystery of Being* (1951).

While Sartre was enjoying the liberated air of Paris in 1945, and basking in the success of *Being and Nothingness*, which made him an overnight celebrity, an Englishman with a French mother, A. J. Ayer, argued that Sartre's ideas were nonsense from start to finish.

[Sartre's] metaphysical pessimism which is well in the existentialist tradition, is no doubt appropriate for our time, but I do not think it is logically well founded. In particular Sartre's reasoning on the subject of *le néant* seems to me exactly on a par with that of the king in *Alice through the Looking-Glass*. 'I see nobody on the road,' said Alice. 'I only wish that I had such eyes,' remarked the king . . . Whatever may be the effective value of these statements, I cannot but think that they are literally nonsensical.

A. J. Ayer, 'Novelist-Philosopher v. Jean-Paul Sartre',

Horizon (Summer 1945)

The fate of analytic philosophy

Sensing that the Cambridge-based school of analytic philosophy influenced by Russell and Moore (but not so much by Wittgenstein) had run its course, philosophers at Oxford University started a new movement called 'ordinary language' philosophy. The idea – so astonishingly commonsensical that it was, perhaps, obscured from the view of Cambridge philosophers – was that philosophy often got itself into trouble by creating misunderstandings arising from its failure to recognize what words actually meant in everyday use. Frege, Russell and Wittgenstein were concerned with elaborating the rules of language as a logical system; the Oxford philosophers, as they came to be known, were more interested in language as we actually use it. The main members of this group included J. L. Austin (1911–60), Gilbert Ryle (1900–76), H. L. A. Hart (1907–92), and P. F. Strawson (1919–2006).

> What I shall have to say here is neither difficult nor contentious; the only merit I should like to claim for it is that of being true, at least in parts.
>
> J. L. Austin, *How To Do Things With Words* (1962)

P. F. Strawson made his reputation by going nose-to-nose with Bertrand Russell in his 1950 paper 'On Referring' – a direct challenge to Russell's founding document of analytic philosophy, 'On Denoting' (1905) – in which Strawson dismisses Russell's theory of descriptions as 'unquestionably wrong' and 'mistaken'. Strawson used his work on language to re-establish metaphysics in British philosophy, an avenue of inquiry that had largely been killed off by Russell and Moore. However, by metaphysics Strawson meant something very different from what was generally understood by his continental colleagues. He invented two new categories for describing metaphysics: revisionary and descriptive (and it is the latter that he advocates). He says that 'Descriptive metaphysics is content to describe the actual structure of our thought about the world, revisionary metaphysics is concerned to produce a better structure' (*Individuals: An Essay in Descriptive Metaphysics*, 1959). Strawson characterizes Descartes, Leibniz, and Berkeley as revisionary metaphysicians. Hume and Kant are descriptive (although Hume is both revisionary and descriptive, depending on his mood). Strawson likes revisionary metaphysics because their results can be 'permanently interesting', but ultimately they are flawed by the 'intensity of their partial vision'. On the other hand, descriptive metaphysics 'needs no justification at all beyond that of inquiry in general'.

> An analysis, I suppose, may be thought of as a kind of breaking down or decomposing of something. So we have the picture of a kind of intellectual taking to pieces of ideas or concepts; the discovering of what elements a concept or idea is composed and how they are related.
>
> P. F. Strawson, *Analysis and Metaphysics: An Introduction* (1992)

J. L. Austin proposed various models for analysing speech acts, which the American John Searle (*b.*1932) described as language *expressed in the act of speaking* (as opposed to words viewed merely as symbols). In *Speech Acts* (1969) Searle argued that 'The unit of linguistic communication is not, as has generally been supposed, the symbol, word or sentence, or even the token of the symbol, word or sentence in the performance of the speech act'; rather, speech acts 'are the basic or minimal units of linguistic communication'. An important part of Searle's work has been to synthesize contributions on this subject from various thinkers in the analytic tradition, including Wittgenstein and Strawson.

A new direction in the philosophy of mind arose from ordinary language philosophy in the work of Gilbert Ryle. Ryle famously described Cartesian mind-body dualism in *The Concept of Mind* (1949) as the problem of the 'ghost in the machine'. In Cartesian mind-body dualism the body is viewed as substance and the mind as a separate 'immaterial' substance. Ryle developed a theory of language based on the identification of what he called a *category mistake* at the heart of Cartesian dualism. The error lies in using the concept of substance to describe the dispositions and capacities that define 'mind'. Ryle gave as an example of a category mistake the question a foreign tourist might pose when visiting Oxford: 'Where is the university?' The university, of course, does not exist in a single building or campus, but rather in the purpose that unifies a large number of colleges and buildings. Unusually for a British philosopher, Ryle started his career studying the work of Husserl and Heidegger. He even gave lectures on phenomenology at Oxford – to which no one came.

> I want to explain how certain essential parts of mind, language
> and social reality work and how they form a coherent whole.
>
> John Searle, *Mind, Language and Society:*
> *Philosophy in the Real World* (1998)

The American Donald Davidson (1917–2003) elaborated a standard of meaning adequate to ordinary language (what he calls natural language) based on a theory of truth he developed from the work of the Polish logician and mathematician Alfred Tarski (1901–83): 'It must be possible to give a constructive account of the meaning of the sentences of the language. Such an account I call a theory of meaning for the language, and I suggest that a theory of meaning that conflicts with this condition, whether put forward by philosopher, linguist or psychologist, cannot be a theory of a natural language' ('Theories of Meaning and Learnable Languages', 1964).

The most original American thinking in the philosophy of language is that of Noam Chomsky (*b*.1928), the inventor of generative and transformational grammar. In *Syntactic Structures* (1957) Chomsky sought to identify the logical structures of grammar. He found that relations such as subject and object are not absolute, but relative, and exist beneath our use of language in what he called 'deep structures'. In transformational grammar all utterances have a syntax, which Chomsky calls 'a context-free grammar extended with transformational rules'. The value of the transformational grammar model of language is that it allowed Chomsky to show how a speaker who possesses a finite set of terms and rules of grammar has the possibility to speak and comprehend an infinite number of utterances. In the latter part of his career, Chomsky has been rather less famous as a philosopher of language than as a vocal critic of US foreign policy and for his position as America's most prominent left-wing public intellectual.

Chomsky is famous for proposing that beneath every sentence in the mind of a speaker is an invisible, inaudible deep structure, the interface to the mental lexicon. The deep structure is converted by transformational rules into a surface structure that corresponds more closely to what is pronounced and heard. The rationale is that certain constructions, if they were listed in the mind as surface structures, would have to be multiplied out in thousands of redundant variations that would have to have been learned one by one, whereas if the constructions were listed as deep structures, they would be simple, few in number, and economically learned.

Steven Pinker, *Words and Rules* (1999)

The Vienna Circle's concern with language was an early interest of the American Willard V. Quine, who moved beyond logical positivism to develop a holistic approach to knowledge. Quine was the most prominent advocate of scientism – the view that science can explain most things: for Quine philosophy is science and vice versa. In a paper entitled 'Two Dogmas of Empiricism' (1951) he rejected the distinction between analytic and synthetic propositions, which is central to logical positivism. In *Word and Object* (1960) he developed his thesis of the 'indeterminacy of translation', arguing that there can be no single, correct 'translation' of a subject's utterances, even within his own language.

As the twentieth century neared its end, some of analytic philosophy's leading lights developed views that sometimes appeared to have elements in common with continental thought, and which re-embraced metaphysics as useful for philosophy. The Serbian-American philosopher of mind Thomas Nagel (*b*.1937) argues that mind and the subjective experience of being cannot be adequately explained by physics ('What Is It Like to Be a Bat?', 1974). T. S. Kuhn (1922–96) argued in *The Structure of Scientific Revolutions* (1962) that scientists cannot separate their subjectivity from their work, and that changes in scientific paradigms do not occur in a neat orderly progression from one idea to the next, but through a violent eruption caused by a new way of conceptualizing the world. Quine's student Hilary Putnam (*b*.1926) further underlined the complexity of logical and mathematical understanding by claiming that mathematics is not purely logical in its foundations, but 'quasi'-empirical, because it must take account of scientific method to find agreement among investigators.

As the early agenda of analytic thought became exhausted, its practitioners have returned to the branches of philosophy that exercised Plato and Aristotle: logic, politics, ethics and aesthetics. The English philosopher of mathematics Michael Dummett (*b.*1925) and the American philosopher and logician Saul Kripke (*b.*1940) are leading contemporary practitioners of logic and the philosophy of language, and they have also linked these subjects to metaphysics. John Rawls's (1921–2002) treatise *A Theory of Justice* (1971) draws upon the arguments of Hume, Kant, J. S. Mill and Rousseau to establish a theoretical model of fairness for the post-Enlightenment republic.

Ethics – which went through a dry patch after G. E. Moore – found a new lease of life in England in the work of R. M. Hare (1919–2002) and Bernard Williams (1929–2003). Hare's *The Language of Morals* (1952) and Williams's *Ethics and the Limits of Philosophy* (1985) provided fresh impetus to British ethics. The Scottish-born philosopher Alasdair MacIntyre (*b.*1929) started life as a Marxist, but converted to Roman Catholicism. His *After Virtue* (1981) seeks to reintroduce an Aristotelian teleological approach to late twentieth century ethics.

> If we were to ask of a person 'What are his moral principles?' the way in which we could be most sure of a true answer would be by studying what he *did*.
>
> R. M. Hare, *The Language of Morals* (1952)

In aesthetics – a field left largely unexplored by analytic philosophy in the modern period, with the notable exception of George Santayana – the Americans Arthur C. Danto (*b*.1924) and Stanley Cavell (*b*.1926) have been pre-eminent. Both have brokered a kind of rapprochement with continental philosophy, in that Danto has appealed to Hegel's aesthetics and Merleau-Ponty's theory of perception, while Cavell cites Heidegger among his influences.

Cavell and Danto are good examples of the widening of the agenda of post-analytic American philosophy. But of all late twentieth-century Americans, Richard Rorty's (1931–2007) philosophical journey best represents the variety of tendencies that are available to American philosophy today. A student of Rudolf Carnap at the University of Chicago, Rorty would turn away from analytic philosophy to forge his own brand of pragmatism – that most American of philosophies – informed by Hegel, Darwin and Dewey. A close reader of Heidegger and Wittgenstein, Rorty arrived at an original critique of language and epistemology in *Philosophy and the Mirror of Nature* (1979).

In this book Rorty challenged two cornerstones of empiricism:

the representational theory of perception, and the correspondence theory of truth. The first says that the mind acts in such a way as to mirror what exists in nature (as Descartes, Locke and Kant argued); the second says that 'truth' is in agreement with 'reality', which is to say that statements we make correspond to actual states of affairs (i.e., 'the way things are'). Rorty says that 'truths' elicited in this fashion are simply the result of tricks we do with language to get the result we want. This calls into question the raison d'être of analytic philosophy: because its alleged 'problems' are the result of language games, its results are of interest only to people who play such games. Rorty was not one of those people. He gave up his chair in philosophy and spent the rest of his life in a department of Humanities.

Nothing requires us to first get straight about language, then about belief and knowledge, then about personhood, and finally about society. There is no such thing as 'first philosophy' – neither metaphysics nor philosophy of language nor philosophy of science. But, once again and for the last time, that claim about philosophy itself is just one more terminological suggestion made on behalf of the same cause, the cause of providing contemporary liberal culture with a vocabulary which was suited to the needs of former days.

Richard Rorty, *Contingency, Irony and Solidarity* (1989)

German philosophy remakes itself

Post-war German philosophy underwent a gradual rehabilitation, and followed three main strands: the neo-Marxism of the Frankfurt School; a new hermeneutics typified by Hans-Georg Gadamer (1900–2002); and a re-evaluation of 'the Enlightenment project' by the neo-Marxist social philosopher Jürgen Habermas (*b*.1929), who, while being a leading member of the Frankfurt School, also distances himself from it.

Gadamer, along with Arendt and Herbert Marcuse (1898–1979), was among Heidegger's most successful students. Unlike Arendt and Marcuse, Gadamer was not a Jew and did not have to flee Germany; in fact, he signed a 1933 document supporting Hitler and his leadership (though he later claimed to be a 'political innocent' who didn't know what he was doing). Gadamer's main achievement in restoring hermeneutics to the forefront of philosophy was to question how meaning arises in language. Gadamer argued that we *are* language: we exist *in* it and through our use of it.

For Gadamer, hermeneutics *is* philosophy. In *Truth and Method* (1960) he looked beyond the recent tendency towards specialization and back to the glory days of German idealism with its *Wissenschaftslehre* or entire 'science of knowledge'. Both Gadamer and his fellow hermeneuticist, the Frenchman Paul Ricoeur (1913–

2005), posited that epistemology should not only embrace the points of view of individual human subjects, but must also acknowledge that prejudice (or pre-judging) plays a role in the acquisition of knowledge. Additionally, Gadamer argues, all human understanding occurs in an historical context that affects the ontology of the interpreter and the text. He regards these factors as liberating rather than limiting. His understanding of history and meaning is expressed in the concept of the *fusion of horizons*, in which past and present, 'old and new are always combining into something of living value'.

Jürgen Habermas, perhaps the last member of the Frankfurt School, is the proponent of a tendency he calls *communicative rationality* in the political arena (which he refers to as the 'public sphere'). Habermas's main focus is on continuing what he calls the 'Enlightenment project'. He wants to ground philosophy, politics and the law in the eighteenth-century principles of reason espoused by Kant and later by Hegel and Marx. (Indeed, Habermas's connection with those thinkers is so strong that, while reading him, one has the feeling they are in the room with us, that they are a vital part of the dialogue that Habermas is attempting to excite in us). Habermas defines the public sphere as places where rational dialogue can occur, and this dialogue is conceived by Habermas as communicative rationality, a concept he elaborates in *The Theory of Communicative Action* (1981).

> Only with the establishment of the bourgeois constitutional state and the legalization of a political public sphere was the press as a forum of rational-critical debate released from the pressure to take sides ideologically; now it could abandon its polemical stance and concentrate on the profit opportunities for a commercial business.
>
> Jürgen Habermas, *The Structural Transformation of the Public Sphere: An Inquiry into a Category of Bourgeois Society* (1962) (trans. Thomas Burger, 1989)

Habermas's position is opposed to that of the French philosopher Michel Foucault (1926–84). In fact, Habermas accused Foucault of relativism – in effect, amorality – after reading the Frenchman's meditations on the theme of power. Foucault resisted categorization as a post-structuralist or any other type of philosopher. If he worked in a tradition, he argued, it was that of Nietzsche, the great thinker of *On the Genealogy of Morals* (1887). Foucault saw the world as being constructed by various *discourses of power* – whether those of the Church, the state or philosophy itself. There is no objectively constituted history, he argued. What we think of as 'history' is in reality a series of histories that are the product of larger forces beyond the control of (or even the cognizance of) the subject. Indeed, for Foucault, history is the identification and description of discourses of power behind the operations of social control over populations at various moments and places in time. It is by turning things upside down (inverting the role of the subject) and posing questions in alternative ways that Foucault can be said to be a Nietzschean.

Foucault's *Madness and Civilization* (1961) broke with the new orthodoxies of phenomenology and existentialism to offer an original analysis of how society viewed (or created) 'madness' at different moments in history. Thus, madness moves from its revered status as divine ecstasy in the classical period to its post-Enlightenment manifestation as a medical diagnosis of an illness that must be treated: segregated, confined, drugged. Foucault's genius was to combine aspects of various theoretical sources and fashion tools for his own use. In *The Order of Things* (1966) he elicited the linguistic structures (epistemes) that lie behind the organization of academic disciplines and official knowledge, and showed that 'progress' from one period and its epistemes to another is not always a smooth, evolutionary process, but may be characterized as a rupture known as an 'epistemic break' (of the sort described by the American physicist-philosopher Thomas S. Kuhn in *The Structure of Scientific Revolutions*). Foucault's last work was a projected four-volume study of human sexuality of which three have been published: *The Will to Knowledge* (1976), *The Use of Pleasure* (1984) and *The Care of the Self* (1984). In *The Will to Knowledge* Foucault rejects the 'repressive hypothesis' which argues that sexuality is driven underground and out of sight by repressive regimes, such as Victorian morality. On the contrary, he argues, any attempts at repression lead to discourses that emphasize rather than repress sexuality. In *The Use of Pleasure* he revisits classical Greece to explore its tolerance for – indeed, celebration of – a full range of sexual practices. In *The Care of the Self*, Foucault moves towards a description of how the Christian tradition has led to our domination by the 'sciences of sexuality'. Foucault was an early victim of AIDS, from which he died in 1984.

A post-structural world

Philosophers like Foucault attract the attention of a much wider audience than brilliant analytic philosophers like Michael Dummett or Hilary Putnam, because they focus on areas that interest the general reading public – the nature of knowledge or history or sexuality – rather than on technical areas of philosophy such as logic, of which a general audience has no knowledge. In France, the dominant strand of contemporary philosophy that supplanted existentialism in the early 1960s was structuralism. It began (like its analytic cousins) as a rather technical analysis of how language works and our relation to it, but structuralism was soon appropriated by thinkers who referred to themselves as structuralists, and then later as post-structuralists. They wanted to explain not only the phenomena of everyday life, but also to answer perennial metaphysical questions, such as 'What does it mean *to be*?', 'What do we mean when we say "I"?', and 'What is the status of objects in our world?'

The difference between structuralism and existentialism is simple: the world-constituting 'I' of existentialism is displaced by the linguistic relation between signifier and signified. In the philosophy of Sartre, Sartre believes that Sartre is speaking. In the work of the Swiss linguist Ferdinand de Saussure, Saussure might have viewed himself as *a place where language occurs*. Saussure's simple but revolutionary discovery was that language is not a set of fixed words with unambiguous meanings, but a system of signs in which the connection between signifier and signified is always arbitrary. These ideas are elaborated in his *Course in General Linguistics* (1916).

Linguistics has very close connections with other sciences. Sometimes they provide linguistics with data and sometimes linguistics provides them with data. The boundaries between linguistics and its neighbouring sciences are not always clearly drawn. For example, linguistics must be carefully distinguished from ethnography and prehistory, both of them disciplines in which linguistic facts may be utilized as evidence. It must likewise be distinguished from anthropology, which studies mankind as a species; whereas language is a social phenomenon.

Ferdinand de Saussure, *Course in General Linguistics* (1916)

(trans. Roy Harris, 1983)

Saussure conceives language as a series of dualities. The most important of these is the *signifier* and the *signified*, which are not related to one another in any absolute, pre-ordained way that refers to any pre-determined meaning. Their relationship is quite the opposite: it is arbitrary. Saussure further defined the concepts of *langue* and *parole*: *langue* being the language as it might be contained in a dictionary, *parole* being the way in which it is used by speakers. Language, Saussure argues, is 'a system of signs that express ideas'. Meaning arises in the play of signifier and signified, leading to polyvalence (a multiplicity of possible meanings). The destruction of fixed meaning in language caused a re-examination of conventionally held assumptions in epistemology and ontology, which led to post-structuralism (and, some would say, a dangerous relativism).

The usefulness of Saussure's discovery is that the metaphor of *a language* could be applied to virtually any investigation, thus giving us concepts such as the '*grammar* of film' to talk about the operation of narratives in movies. Saussure's conception of language as a system provided a model for two important investigators: the French anthropologist Claude Lévi-Strauss (1908–2009) and his compatriot Roland Barthes (1915–80), a semiotician who regarded the whole world as a 'text'.

Lévi-Strauss's anthropological work *Tristes Tropiques* (1955) was among the first to use structuralism as a methodological tool in a field other than linguistics. He tested its general utility by applying it to the problem of the 'savage mind', discovering that the savage mind uses the same thought processes as the 'civilized' mind. He borrowed Saussure's concepts of *langue* and *parole* to outline a theory of structuralist anthropology.

If Nietzsche proclaimed the death of God, then Roland Barthes announced the death of the subject. In his essay 'The Death of the Author' (1967) Barthes claimed that authors were not the creators of texts, readers were. Barthes used the arbitrary relation of the signifier to the signified to develop a methodology that exposed a multitude of hidden factors at work in any of the representations that he called 'texts'. In *Mythologies* (1957) he elaborated a method for decoding 'texts' (be they advertisements for wine, magazine covers or the works of Balzac) to reveal their hidden meaning.

> In modern texts, the voices are so treated that any reference is impossible: the discourse, or better, the language, speaks: nothing more.
>
> Roland Barthes, *S/Z* (1970) (trans. Richard Miller, 1974)

The French psychoanalyst Jacques Lacan (1901–81) took the ideas of Saussure and Barthes to create a post-structuralist position which claimed that the unconscious is structured like a language, and that the 'I' is located outside itself, in language. Lacan published very little, preferring to present the results of his research in weekly seminars at the École normale supérieure and then at the Sorbonne between 1953 and 1980. Transcripts of these seminars have appeared as *Écrits*, a series of publications that began in 1977. Using the lecture format, Lacan built up the structure of his ideas, leaving a wake of discarded hypotheses. Like the lectures of Wolff, Bergson and William James in earlier times, Lacan's talks drew a large crowd of the brilliant, the curious and the fashionable.

Unfortunately, Lacan's thought uses so many neologisms and obscure references it seems designed to elude all but the most learned. He draws heavily upon the history of philosophy after Aristotle, and there are those from whom he takes bricks to build his own edifice – Hegel, Jaspers, Heidegger; and those he rejects, defining himself against them – Mill and Bentham, for instance. To give just one example of Lacan's difficulty, he answers the question, 'What am *I*?' as if it were '*Where* am I?', to which he replies: '*I* am in the place from which "the universe is a flaw in the purity of Non-Being" is vociferated.' A certain amount of dedication is required to follow Lacan.

The French-Algerian philosopher Jacques Derrida (1930–2004) made use of the work of Husserl and Heidegger, along with that of the structuralists, to create a method called *deconstruction* in which he explored the territory that lay beyond Barthes's 'death of the author'. Of all late modern philosophers, Derrida is the most controversial. To his followers, deconstructionism is a powerful tool for getting at the root causes of ideas and misunderstandings; to his (mainly, though not exclusively, analytic) critics, it is nothing but smoke and mirrors, and he is not worthy of being called a philosopher.

A deconstruction would involve the demonstration that for presence to function as it is said to, it must have the qualities that supposedly belong to its opposite, absence. Thus, instead of defining absence in terms of presence, as *its* negation, we can treat 'presence' as the effect of a generalized absence or, as we shall see shortly, of *différance*.

Jonathan Culler, *On Deconstruction: Theory and Criticism after Structuralism* (1982)

Derrida complained that Western thought had privileged the spoken word above the written text at least since the time of Plato (Socrates was a talker, not a writer). In *Speech and Phenomena* (1967) Derrida begins his attack on this over-valuing of the spoken word by beginning to describe how it is that we speak, and what role speech plays in relation to how we constitute ourselves, and our understanding of ourselves as temporal beings. When we speak, there is an infinitesimal lag between the speech utterance and our hearing of what we just said. What we hear ourselves saying already belongs to the past, but we fold it into our present, while at the same time looking forward to the future, which, in the blink of an eye, is already the past. This hiatus that separates us from ourselves is *différance*, a term that Derrida first used in his 1963 paper 'Cogito and the History of Madness'. In this early work he identifies this gap or delay, this *différance*, as similar to the constitutive lag that occurs when we see 'ourselves' in a mirror. There is a hesitation, a moment of recognition, and then a kind of identification with the reflection that is a part of our self-constitution, or *auto-affection*, as Derrida describes it (borrowing from Aristotle's definition of God as 'thought thinking itself'). The example just given is of Derrida criticizing a text by Husserl, and is an instance of deconstruction at work. It is in terms of deconstructions of our experience that Derrida views himself – and us. Our history has been one of our 'I' as an acting subject (as in the author of Augustine's *Confessions*) maturing in the *cogito* of Descartes, and perfected in the transcendental idealism of Kant and Husserl. However, I have – it has – become progressively de-centred starting with the structuralism of Saussure and ending in the de-centred 'I' of Derrida's deconstructionism.

> By virtue of its innermost intention, and like all questions
> about language, structuralism escapes the classical history
> of ideas which already supposes structuralism's possibility,
> for the latter naively belongs to the province of language
> and propounds itself within it.
>
> Jaccques Derrida, *Writing and Difference* (1967)
>
> (trans. Alan Bass, 1978)

It is said by Derrida's critics that his work is unintelligible. At the very least, one must agree that it can be very dense. But Derrida, like Nietzsche, is also a playful writer, and one must be alive to this aspect of his work to appreciate its originality. In *Glas* (1974), for instance, he has fun presenting texts concerning Hegel and the French novelist Jean Genet (1910–86) alongside one another on the page, mimicking the style of Genet's essay 'What Remains of a Rembrandt Torn into Four Equal Pieces and Flushed Down the Toilet' (1967). So a sense of humour – the sort that Socrates might hope for – is essential to read Derrida. As is an encyclopaedic knowledge of Western thought, in particular the technical requirements of phenomenology.

When critics complained that Derrida's work is unintelligible, he would argue that it is because they do not speak the language; they are unfamiliar with the subject matter and terminology of the Western tradition, which includes the long line of thinkers descending from Kant through Hegel to Derrida. In this sense analytic and continental philosophers sometimes find themselves in a dialogue of the deaf: the former are intent on finding certainty in logical or linguistic foundations, while the latter (or Derrideans, at least) have demonstrated that this cannot be done. For Derrida there is no pessimism or nihilism in this understanding; it simply makes him especially alert to the language we use, and also the fact that philosophers need to define themselves against non-philosophers.

Julia Kristeva (*b.*1941) represents in her gender, nationality and varied philosophical interests a kind of diversity that may eventually help to render the old analytic–continental divide a thing of the past. Just as many of the early analytic philosophers fled Nazi Germany to become British or American nationals, Kristeva left communist Bulgaria to become a naturalized French citizen. Like Hannah Arendt – whose work she discusses in *Hannah Arendt* (1999) – Kristeva is deeply influenced by Heidegger, and both women studied Christianity: Arendt's thesis was *Love and St Augustine*, while a recent book of Kristeva's is *This Incredible Need to Believe* (2006). Both women were also deeply influenced by the phenomenology of Edmund Husserl. And they both emphasized the life force as having primacy over Heidegger's being-towards-death. Arendt called it *natality*; Kristeva adds the concept of the *chora*. Where the two differ is in relation to Freud and psychoanalysis, which Arendt rejected, but Kristeva embraced (she is, in addition to being a philosopher and novelist, a practising psycho-analyst).

The abject has only one quality of the object – that of being opposed to I.

Julia Kristeva, *Powers of Horror: An Essay on Abjection* (1980) (trans. Leon S. Roudiez, 1982)

Lacan was a strong influence on Kristeva, who seeks to locate subjectivity amid the debris of a post-empirical, post-analytic, post-post-structuralist world. In this quest Kristeva discovers there are many subjectivities: masculine, feminine, stranger, psychotic, and as many sexualities as there are people.

For Kristeva, human subjectivity is wholly grounded in the body, and she finds its ultimate manifestations in language, especially the primordial, physical articulations of language. She is particularly interested in the physical efforts that result in sound, but which have their origins prior to the rules of a language, prior to the paternal origins described by Freud. These origins, according to Kristeva, are located in the maternal, in the subject's pre-natal experience. All of us, irrespective of sex, learn the rhythm of life, the music of being, in the womb. Separation from the womb and birth into a world dominated by the institutions of paternalism alienate the female subject. As a result, her experiences, actions and utterances are different from those of men.

Borrowing the term from Plato (just as Arendt borrowed heavily from the Greeks), Kristeva uses *chora* to describe our pre-linguistic experience, which is maternal, because much of it occurs at the foetal stage of our development. She argues that even after the child acquires language, with its paternally dominated system of signs, this maternal, pre-linguistic self that was established in the context of the *chora* remains with us. It is a wild, untamable thing. It finds its ultimate expression in poetic language, which challenges the prison walls of linguistic rules. American feminists have rejected Kristeva, because she locates so much significance in the maternal, in contrast to Beauvoir, who denounced motherhood in *The Second Sex*. (Ironically, Kristeva is a co-founder of the Simone de Beauvoir Prize, for work in human rights.)

Kristeva is responsible for introducing two important terms into popular intellectual discourse: *intertextuality* and *abjection*. Intertextuality has become a fundamental element of post-structuralist theory; it refers to the way in which one text informs another by a reader's reading history, or by authors' direct or indirect references to one another. In *Revolution in Poetic Language* (1974) Kristeva identified intertextuality with characteristic clarity as the 'transposition of one (or several) sign-system(s) into another'. She develops Saussure's idea of polyvalence (see p.232) to arrive at a new conclusion: 'If one grants that every signifying practice is a field of transpositions of various signifying systems (an intertextuality), one then understands that its "place" of enunciation and its denoted "object" are never single, complete and identical to themselves, but always plural, shattered.'

Kristeva uses *abjection* or the *abject* to describe the condition of the marginalized: women, people of colour, the mentally ill, the criminal. In *Powers of Horror: An Essay on Abjection* (1980) she uses the term to describe the complex situation of the subject who is not simply alienated, but who is 'radically excluded' and drawn 'toward the place where meaning collapses'. In abjection, 'A certain "ego" that merged with its master, a superego, has flatly driven it away. It lies outside, beyond the set, and does not seem to agree to the latter's rules of the game.'

The subject matter of Kristeva's work, like that of most continental philosophers, could not be more different from that of analytic philosophers. The subject matter is the subject – his or her presence or absence; while the analytics' focus is on language as object of logical and linguistic inquiry. A crude way of defining the difference between them is that analytic philosophers study language in itself, while continental philosophers are interested in the things one does with it.

Thinking about the analytic continental divide brings to mind an image of two groups of persons standing apart from one another at the edge of a lake, dressed in bathing costumes. They are peering across the lake, apparently thinking about swimming to the other side.

What is on the other side? The answer is unclear. Knowledge? Danger? Just another shore?

One at a time, the people in group A jump into the lake. Some doggy-paddle, succeeding only in staying in one place. Some make slow progress, with awkward swimming strokes. A couple of them drown. A very few proceed with swift, sure strokes and reach the other side.

The people in group B stand at the shore, some looking down at the ground, some looking behind them, and some looking to the opposite shore, noticing the progress of group A. They begin to argue among themselves. What is meant by swimming? They analyse the verb 'to swim'. They discuss what (or who) is signi-fied if a subject were to undertake the activity of swimming.

The people in group A are continental philosophers. They are determined to cross the water, to go to the unknown place, even at the risk of embarrassing themselves with awkward movements or failure. Group B comprises analytical philosophers. They are careful, precise and safe. Their feet are not in the water, but they have a lot to say about swimming.

Another image: group A is building a bridge, attempting to see how far it can span; group B is digging a mine, trying to see how deep it can go.

In their constant reaching, continental philosophers seem to be searching for an eternally fresh *beginning* in philosophy. (Analytics would say they are overreaching.) Analytic philosophers, with their careful steps and mission of dissolving problems, would appear to want an *end* to philosophy. (Continentals would say that their focus is too narrow.)

To the non-professional philosopher – that is to say, almost everyone in the world and most readers of this book – the differences between the two groups sometimes appear more like postures or poses struck, rather than thoughtful positions convincingly held. At bottom, the two camps have common antecedents; it remains to be seen whether they might rediscover common goals.

AFTERWORD

Philosophy's Future

In *The Grand Design* (2010) the physicist Stephen Hawking declares that *philosophy is dead*. In his view, scientists have taken over the 'real' questions of philosophy and are busy answering them. They will eventually answer every one, leaving philosophy with nothing to do. I'm fifty-six years old, and I've yet to read a sillier remark.

To say that philosophy is dead amounts to saying that thinking is dead. Heidegger teaches us that philosophy *is* thinking, and philosophers do plenty of thinking about science. Indeed, the *philosophy of science* is one area that has grown dramatically since W. V. Quine questioned logical positivism and T. S. Kuhn identified the means by which scientific paradigms rise and fall. Einstein himself was directly influenced by Kant's work on the subjectivity of the observer; and the work of Einstein and others on wave-particle duality has affected the way today's philosophers think about what we can know and how we can know it.

Philosophers continue to teach us things that science alone cannot. Consider, for instance, the *rise of the subject*, from its appearance in the *Confessions* of St Augustine to its proclaiming of the *cogito* in Descartes, to its world-making role in Kantian idealism, its essence-constituting self in Husserl, and its existential, useless-passion-of-a-self in Sartre . . . And then consider the *decline of the subject*: just as God came under attack prior to His death being declared by Nietzsche, so the subject was similarly assaulted. Saussure showed that language (and everything else) has no fixed, subject-determined meaning, but that significance arises in the space between signifier and signified; then Barthes declared the death of the author; and Derrida deconstructed language until there was no ground left to stand on. We learned that language uses us rather than the other way around.

In the early twenty-first century Julia Kristeva, borrowing tools from the Greeks, phenomenologists, existentialists, hermeneuticists, structuralists, post-structuralists, Marx, Freud, Lacan and Derrida, forges a new set of tools with which she attempts to understand the dilemmas we face today, in an age marked by diversity in gender, ethnicity and nationality. At the same time, pursuing a different path in philosophy, Saul Kripke refines modal logic in a way that not only informs our understanding of language, but which is also important for computer science.

So, philosophers have been busy.

But what will they be busy doing later in the twenty-first century, and beyond? J. L. Austin said the Greeks had identified about a thousand philosophical problems, and that, after Wittgenstein, most of them were on the way to being solved. A. J. Ayer said that the work of solving philosophical problems was nearly done. But John Searle disagrees. 'I would estimate that about 90 per cent of the philosophical problems left us by the Greeks are still with us,' he says in his essay 'The Future of Philosophy' (1999), 'and that we have not yet found a scientific, linguistic or mathematical way to answer them.'

The besetting sin of philosophers seems to be throwing the baby out with the bathwater. From the beginning, each 'new wave' of philosophers has simply ignored the insights of the previous wave in the course of advancing its own. Today we stand near the end of a century in which there has been an unprecedented forgetting of the insights of previous centuries and millennia.

Hilary Putnam, *The Threefold Cord: Mind, Body and World* (1999)

So, still a job to do – especially for those who think that the 90 per cent of problems is amenable to scientific, linguistic or mathematical solution. But Husserl and Bergson, both of them renowned mathematicians, did not think that methodologies based on mathematics or linguistics were the right tools for solving all of the major problems of the modern period. The impasse between analytic and continental philosophy, which began when Frege and Husserl parted (and when Russell, Moore and Wittgenstein followed Frege; and Heidegger, Gadamer and Derrida followed Husserl), still remains.

Understanding the full range of questions that exercised philosophers in the past can provide clues to how present and future problems might be solved. The problem of terrorism raises important questions about belief and reason – our starting point in this book. How can dialogue be possible between the fundamentalist point of view and a post-Enlightenment one? Our responses to terrorism – pre-emptive war, the use of torture, ignoring international frontiers in pursuit of those we deem our enemies – cry out for philosophical study and guidance. Can civilian casualties ever be justified? Or indefinite detention without habeas corpus? What does the 'war on terror' mean? What is terror? Who is a terrorist? In pursuit of the oft-stated aim of protecting its cherished values and hard-won freedoms from the assault of illiberal extremists, should the West resort to using the methods of its enemies? And if so, how does that affect us? In order to protect our civil liberties should governments restrict our civil liberties to combat terrorism?

Globalization raises questions of scarcity for tens of millions of people around the world. It also impacts on our environment. What is the way to deal with the irrational view that climate change is not occurring? What gives government the right to act in defence of the Earth and its resources? What gives corporations the right to exploit those resources until they are depleted, if environmental disaster and social chaos are the likely outcomes? Medical and health issues, such as abortion, are an arena for fierce and often polarizing ethical debate. Greater human longevity at the start of the twenty-first century has already opened a discussion about the morality of euthanasia. Advances in biotechnology and its associated industries raise other new ethical questions; for instance, is it right to copyright (and sell) the naturally occurring DNA structure of an organism? To what extent is the genetic modification of humans and other species good or bad? Nuclear war has now threatened humankind for more than sixty-five years, and while the end of the Cold War has reduced the likelihood of a nuclear conflict between nations, most experts believe that a crude nuclear device will be used by terrorists within the lifetime of those reading this book. Add to this a long list of unsolved problems of a purely philosophical (logical or mathematical) nature, and there is enough to keep philosophers busy for a very long time.

> Practically every university throughout the world deems it as essential to have a philosophy department as to have a history department or a chemistry department. This is certainly a very lucky thing for philosophers.
>
> Michael Dummett, *The Nature and Future of Philosophy*
>
> (2010)

The teaching of philosophy, the writing of philosophy, and the constant task of evaluating and re-evaluating the history of philosophy, is a job that will always need to be done. Most of the thinkers mentioned in this book were not superstars like Jean-Paul Sartre and Simone de Beauvoir. Most spent their lives working diligently in universities (not always in philosophy departments), and many of them were known only to their students and their peers in the field. But their contributions have been crucial to the liberal arts, and to knowledge for its own sake. Today university education is becoming more and more specialized, and directed at specific vocational skills, rather than a general understanding of the world that can be applied in a multiplicity of settings after graduation. Perhaps more than ever before, we need philosophy. The world can only improve if it is inhabited by people whose minds are agile; who take delight in understanding the arguments of others, and pride in making themselves better understood.

A Note to the Reader

Readers who are sufficiently curious to delve deeper into the history of Western philosophy might wish to consult my forthcoming book *Fifty Thinkers Who Shaped the Modern World*. It begins with Immanuel Kant as a starting point for the modern period, and ends with Julia Kristeva, the Bulgarian-French polymath whose work is informed by so much of the history of philosophy described herein, and whose own work points to new destinations for twenty-first-century thought.

Acknowledgements

Peg Culver, director of the Bancroft Public Library in Salem, NY provided impeccable service in procuring dozens of books, and was a constant companion during the making of this book. She was ably assisted by Susan Getty, Rebecca Brown, and Julie Brown.

The following people helped in many ways for which I am grateful: Dave Allison; Babette Babbich, Professor of Philosophy, Fordham University; Jürgen Braungardt, psychotherapist, Oakland, CA; Al Budde and Nancy Flint-Budde; Charles Carlson, Department of Philosophy, Texas A&M University; Felicia Dougherty; Professor Sigrid Close, Department of Astronautics and Aeronautics, Stanford University; Nancy Fitzpatrick; Hans Herlof Grelland, Professor of Quantum Chemistry (Physics) and Philosophy, University of Agder; Professor Pete Gunter, University of North Texas Department of Philosophy and Religion; Laureen Jean Harrington;

Dr Charles Krecz, Department of Philosophy, University of Texas at Austin; Irma Kurtz; Professor Leonard Lawlor, Department of Philosophy, Pennsylvania State University; Dr Jon McGinnis, Department of Philosophy, University of Missouri at St Louis; Professor David Mowry, University Distinguished Teaching Professor, SUNY Plattsburgh; William L. McBride, Arthur G. Hansen Distinguished Professor of Philosophy, Purdue University; John J. McDermott, Distinguished Professor of Philosophy and Humanities, Texas A&M University; Dr Paul Nnodim, Associate Professor, Department of Philosophy, Massachusetts College of Liberal Arts; Rabbi Norman and Naomi Patz; Beth Rabinove; Gila Reinstein; Fred & Norene Russo; Beth Steves; Glenn Stokem; Sean Sayers, Professor of Philosophy, University of Kent; Matthew Silliman, Professor of Philosophy, Massachusetts College of Liberal Arts; Dr Caren Steinlight; Dr Stephen Steinlight; Dr Robin Waterfield.

I am grateful to the following university and public libraries for providing books through interlibrary loan: Clifton Park-Halfmoon Public Library; College of Saint Rose; Crandall Public Library, Glens Falls, NY; Gloversville NY Free Library; New York State Library; Rensselaer Polytechnic Institute Library; Saratoga Springs Public Library; Schenectady Public Library; Skidmore College Library; SUNY Albany; SUNY Plattsburgh; SUNY Stony Brook, Union College Library; Waterford Public Library.

Warm thanks go to my agent Anthony Sheil. At Aitken Alexander I am indebted to Liv Stones, Imogen Pelham, and Joaquim Ferandes. Richard Milbank commissioned this book for Atlantic, and has been a wonderful companion throughout its production. Ian Pindar did an admirable job of copy editing, and I thank him for it. Likewise Alan Rutter on the index. Atlantic CEO Toby Mundy is a great friend whose support and good counsel I have enjoyed for several decades.

Bibliographical Note

Inevitably, when writing a book of this nature a great debt is owed to others, beyond the obvious business of preparing a bibliography. In my case, I owe an enormous amount to my philosophy tutors David Mowry and Charles Krecz, and to my thesis supervisor Roger Poole. When I was a young man my mother gave me Father Frederick Copleston's nine-volume *A History of Philosophy* (1947–74) and I think it probably had a much greater impact on me than I ever realized.

It is a daunting task writing a history of Western philosophy – even a very short one – and every time I embarked on descriptions of things with which I assumed was familiar, I soon found myself in deep water and in need of help.

In my efforts to understand the analytic–continental divide, I am grateful to Babette Babich for her essay 'On the "Analytic-

Continental" Divide in Philosophy: Nietzsche and Heidegger On Truth, Lies and Language' (Prometheus/Humanity Books, 2003), which I heartily recommend to anyone interested in the subject. Hans-Johann Glock's *What is Analytic Philosophy?* (Cambridge University Press, 2008) answers many questions, while explaining what the author thinks is wrong with continental philosophy.

In revisiting ancient philosophy I was delighted to discover Robin Waterfield's *The First Philosophers: The Presocratics and the Sophists* (Oxford University Press, 2000), and I am grateful to him for having answered several queries. In attempting to describe how Greek philosophy survived the loss of the Greek language I consulted two very up-to-date works: Jonathan Lyons's *The House of Wisdom: How the Arabs Transformed Western Civilization* (Bloomsbury, 2009) and Jim Al- Khalili's *Pathfinders: The Golden Age of Arabic Science* (Allen Lane, 2010). Although scholars are often keen to cite the most recent work in a subject, sometimes earlier works have an enduring power to explain and entertain, and that is the case with A. O. Lovejoy's treatment of the concept of *The Great Chain of Being* (Harvard University Press, 1936) from classical times to the nineteenth century.

Those seeking further information about medieval philosophy could do worse than to consult *The Cambridge History of Later Medieval Philosophy* (Cambridge University Press, 1982), edited by Norman Kretzman, Anthony Kenny and Jan Pinborg, as well as David Luscombe's *Medieval Thought* (Oxford University Press, 1997). It was my great privilege to co-edit *The Fontana Dictionary of Modern Thought* (second edition 1988, third edition 2000) with the late Alan Bullock, a project that proved good preparation for writing this book. Bullock's *The Humanist Tradition in the West* (Thames & Hudson, 1985) is a casually erudite and thoughtful summary of the Renaissance tradition, to which J. H. Plumb's *The Italian Renaissance* (Harper and Row, 1965) is a fine introduction. Basil Willey's *The Seventeenth-Century Background* (Chatto and Windus, 1934) remains a standard work.

With the modern period comes the democritization of philosophy – and an explosion of books about it! In every area imaginable there are hundreds of texts to consider, but I will confine myself to a few that I found particularly helpful. Manfred Kuehn's *Kant: A Biography* (Cambridge University Press, 2001) is not only a good introduction to the man and his thought, but it also gives a taste of the times in which he lived. Howard Caygill's *A Kant Dictionary* (Blackwell, 1995) is an essential work of reference. Robert Hanna's *Kant and the Foundations of Analytic Philosophy* (Oxford University Press, 2001) makes an important contribution to our understanding of how Kant influenced analytic and continental philosophy. Roy Porter's *The Creation of the Modern World: The Untold Story of the British Enlightenment* (Norton, 2000) and David K. Naugle's *Worldview: The History of a Concept*

(William B. Eerdmans, 2002) are excellent windows on eighteenth-century thought. Karl Marx is very well introduced by David McLellan in *Karl Marx: His Life and Thought* (Harper Row, 1973), and briefly summarized in *Karl Marx* (Penguin, 1976). Peter Singer's *Hegel: A Very Short Introduction* (Oxford University Press, 1983) is a masterpiece of concision. Eric Hobsbawm's *Industry and Empire: The Birth of the Industrial Revolution* (Pelican, 1969) is essential background reading for the period. Peter J. Bowler gives a good account of Darwin in *Evolution: The History of an Idea* (University of California Press, 2003), and Freud is very well discussed in Peter Gay's *Freud: A Life for Our Time* (J. M. Dent, 1998). A good introduction to Peirce is Joseph Brent's *Charles Sanders Peirce: A Life* (Indiana University Press, 1993). The history of British idealism is thoroughly discussed in *The Philosophy of F. H. Bradley* by Anthony Manser and Guy Stock (Clarendon Press, 1984).

Analytic philosophy gets an excellent preview in *Frege: An Introduction to the Founder of Modern Analytic Philosophy* (Penguin, 1995) by Anthony Kenny. Ray Monk's two-volume biography not only treats Russell's life brilliantly, but also touches on some of the key themes in analytic philosophy. It also gives an account of Russell's relationships with Moore and Wittgenstein: *Bertrand Russell: The Spirit of Solitude 1872–1921* (Jonathan Cape, 1996) and *Bertrand Russell: The Ghost of Madness 1921–1970* (Jonathan Cape, 2000). Monk's biography of *Ludwig Wittgenstein: The Duty of Genius* (Jonathan Cape, 1990) is a work of genius in itself. Anyone interested in the period in which analytic philosophy was formed might want to look at Paul Fussell's *The Great War and Modern Memory* (Oxford University Press, 1975).

Rüdiger Safranski's biographies do for continental philosophy what Ray Monk's do for analytic philosophy. His *Nietzsche: A Philosophical Biography* (W. W. Norton, 2002) explicates the work, while telling the story of a fascinating and tragic life; his *Martin Heidegger: Between Good and Evil* (Harvard University Press, 1998) does a fine job of explaining complex ideas in the context of a pedestrian life. The situation in German university departments of philosophy during the Nazi period is treated by Hans Sluga in *Heidegger's Crisis: Philosophy and Politics in Nazi Germany* (Harvard University Press, 1993). The relationship between Heidegger and his student Hannah Arendt is an important one for modern philosophy, and is introduced with great sensitivity by Daniel Maier-Katkin in *Stranger from Abroad: Hannah Arendt, Martin Heidegger, Friendship and Forgiveness* (W. W. Norton, 2010). William Barrett's early examination of existentialism, *Irrational Man: A Study in Existential Philosophy* (Mercury Books, 1958), remains a vital text. Leonard Lawlor is superb at tracking the developments of phenomenology, existentialism, and post-structuralism, which he does in two key works: *Derrida and Husserl: The Basic Problem of Phenomenology* (Indiana University Press, 2002), and *Thinking*

Through French Philosophy: The Being of the Question (Indiana University Press, 2003). A revisionist look at Sartre by Annie Cohen-Solal, *Jean-Paul Sartre: A Life* (New Press, 2005), caused a rethink of the status of Sartre and Simone de Beauvoir in the pantheon of French philosophy. Structuralism and post-structuralism are very well explained by Jonathan Culler in *Structuralist Poetics* (Routledge & Kegan Paul, 1975). Stephen Hawking and Leonard Mlodinow's *The Grand Design* (Bantam Press, 2010) inadvertently argues for the importance of philosophy by demonstrating how disappointing thinking about science is when divorced from it.

Index